Chosen Country

Chosen Country

A Rebellion in the West

James Pogue

HENRY HOLT AND COMPANY

NEW YORK

Henry Holt and Company
Publishers since 1866
175 Fifth Avenue
New York, New York 10010
www.henryholt.com

Henry Holt® and 🏛® are registered trademarks
of Macmillan Publishing Group, LLC.

Distributed in Canada by Raincoast
Book Distribution Limited

Library of Congress Cataloging-in-Publication Data

Names: Pogue, James, author.
Title: Chosen country : a rebellion in the West /
  James Pogue.
Description: First edition. | New York : Henry Holt and
  Company, 2018.
Identifiers: LCCN 2017059035 (print) |
  LCCN 2017038369 (ebook) | ISBN 9781250169136
  (Ebook) | ISBN 9781250169129 (hardcover)
Subjects: LCSH: Militia movements—United States. |
  Radicalism—United States. | Government, Resistance
  to—United States. | Malheur National Wildlife Refuge
  (Agency : U.S.)
Classification: LCC HN90.R3 (print) | LCC HN90.R3
  P64 2018 (ebook) | DDC 303.48/4—dc23
LC record available at https://lccn.loc.gov/2017059035

ISBN: 978-1-2501-6912-9

Our books may be purchased in bulk for promotional,
educational, or business use. Please contact your local
bookseller or the Macmillan Corporate and Premium
Sales Department at (800) 221-7945, extension 5442, or
by e-mail at MacmillanSpecialMarkets@macmillan.com.

First Edition 2018

Designed by Karen Minster

Printed in the United States of America

10 9 8 7 6 5 4 3 2 1

Kindly separated by nature and a wide ocean from the exterminating havoc of one quarter of the globe; too high-minded to endure the degradations of the others; possessing a chosen country, with room enough for our descendants to the thousandth and thousandth generation . . .

—Thomas Jefferson, First Inaugural Address

. . . a land flowing with milk and honey; And they came in, and possessed it; but they obeyed not thy voice, neither walked in thy law; they have done nothing of all that thou commandedst them to do: therefore thou hast caused all this evil to come upon them.

—Jeremiah 32:22–23

Chosen Country

CHAPTER 1

The Best People You Could Possibly Imagine

It was snowing the night I got to the refuge. It had snowed for almost the entire drive from Portland, and it was only with some difficulty and by the use of tire chains that I'd made it over Mount Hood and through the desert. The drive to Burns, where I checked into what the clerk told me was the last room at the local Days Inn, had taken eight hours, which is not so much longer than it takes to drive in any direction from the town to a city of any size—by measure of distance from an interstate it is the remotest corner of the lower forty-eight. The snow was six inches deep on the streets and falling fast, and there were hardly any cars on the road aside from deputies' cruisers, bearing the markings of counties from all across Oregon. These reinforcements and the riot of rented SUVs in the parking lot at the Days Inn were the only indication that the little town had become the host of an insurrection, suddenly one of the biggest news stories in the world. The dingy Thai restaurant on the silent main drag was closed, with a sign in the window like something out of a western, reading "Sorry Gone to Bend for Supplies."

I was in bad need of a hamburger, a few beers, and bed before midnight—but before I'd managed to eat or even set foot in my motel room I'd gotten a text from my mom, who was watching CNN. "James," she said, "they're moving all kinds of bulldozers and things out there and it sounds crazy." She asked me to stay in for the night. I hadn't had any service since I hit the mountains and had no idea what was happening, but on the strength of her worry I immediately pulled out my atlas of Oregon and set off on the thirty-mile drive down State Route 205. In the snowstorm and the dark the road was almost indistinguishable from the flat sage rangeland, which in turn was entirely indistinguishable from the Malheur National Wildlife Refuge itself, which I would have never been able to find if it weren't for the dozens of news trucks idling on a little rise at the entrance to the refuge headquarters. I parked, shook out a cigarette, and wandered into the halogen-lit portion of the snowstorm. LaVoy Finicum, who had fashioned himself a spokesman for what was going on, was sitting on a camp chair under a tarp with a cowboy hat on his head and a rifle across his knees, having just finished giving the live interview that would make him famous. "They're not going to just come up to a guy holding a rifle and put cuffs on him," he had said, and when asked what exactly he meant by that he went on. "I have been raised in the country all my life. I love dearly to feel the wind on my face, to see the sunrise, to see the moon in the night. I have no intention of spending any of my days in a concrete box." The message that the occupiers were ready to die before being arrested was reported in papers all over the world.

We greeted each other with a nod. Past him was Jason

Patrick, who was on the phone and smoking a cigarette. I waved to him, and he recognized me and waved back, indicating by sign language that he'd catch up with me when his call was done. He was wearing, as he always did, apparently even in the cold of a desert snowstorm, a cheap and oversize suit jacket, with a baggy, blue button-front shirt and khakis. He had salt-and-pepper hair to match a salt-and-pepper beard and bore a plausible-enough resemblance to a much thicker George Clooney that during the standoff "Clooney" became his radio call sign. Eventually it just became his name. He smoked constantly. A friend of mine who knows him once described him as "the smokingest dude on the whole planet." It's hard to imagine what he must have done during his various stints in jail.

"Hey, man," he said and lit another cigarette. We caught up for a few seconds before my phone rang. It was a friend of his and a friendly acquaintance of mine named Brandon Rapolla, a giant, Guamanian marine whom I had met the same day I met Jason, at a different standoff the previous April. I mentioned to Jason who it was and he asked for my phone. I shrugged and gave it to him. "Sup, bro," he said, and there was a brief exchange while Brandon realized who was talking. "Yeah," Jason said, "I'm just up here watching LaVoy's back now."

A man in fatigues approached and pulled me aside. "You know how dangerous it is here tonight?" he asked. I said I didn't. "They're talking about coming in," he said, giving me to understand that by "they" he meant the FBI. I said I hadn't known that, and he indicated with his head to the north end of the rise where an earth mover was being positioned by some enthusiastic occupiers to block a possible assault party from coming down the icy access road to the refuge headquarters. Beside the access road someone had dropped off about half a cord of dried hardwood, and three or four men holding rifles and wearing camo and balaclavas were standing around in the snow, slowly feeding a fire and watching the gravel lot, where we were standing and where LaVoy was out under his tarp. High above us, in a creaking, steel fire tower, ninety feet high, the shadow of a sniper could be seen pacing. The sat trucks and rented Ford Explorers used by the reporters began pulling out of the front lot, and the feel of the place was intensely dark and paranoid. "There's a drone flying around—watch out for that," the man said. All the people who said they saw it described it as a black object with about a six-foot wing-span. I never saw the drone.

I turned back to Jason, who was now in a biting argument with Brandon on my phone. "You know they're not going to do anything, right?" he said, meaning law enforcement. "They're going to wait and wait and wait and wait."

He went quiet for a moment and there began a long and bitter exchange about how Brandon's militia hadn't shown up yet.

"I would say right back that I'm not happy about the beginning," he said into the phone. There were more words. "You know I don't want to hash that out because I'm not going to lose sleep over it. You have to understand I'm just here."

There was a pause while Brandon talked. "Well, listen," Jason said. "Think of the last sentence of the Declaration of Independence: a strong reliance on divine providence." He paused. "It happened how it happened. There's a bunch of ranchers on board, so get in here."

Brandon spoke for a while, presumably saying something about how poorly equipped the occupiers were to conduct an armed rebellion, because Jason suddenly got angry.

"I'm going to come and motherfuck all you military types," he said. "Because your security ops stuff? In America? It's a bunch of bullshit. All you can do here is stand up with pitchforks and torches and you say fuck no. So just put that fucking shit down, stop playing at GI Joe, and listen to the civilian who knows. We can win, but you guys have to stop buttfucking each other and we'll fix it."

He turned to me and winked. "Especially with those purple panties you wear," he said into the phone. He turned back to me. "See? We're in deep now."

Brandon said something and Jason laughed. "Yeah, well, fucking get here and we'll get *real* deep," he said. "Okay. I'm going to give you back and go see how LaVoy's doing."

I got back on the phone with Brandon, who said he had to work but was planning on coming down in a couple of days. He was obviously conflicted about what was happening, which seemed out of character. He had been at the standoff at the Bundys' family ranch, in 2014, and he had been the "head of security" at the militia standoff where I'd met him, the year before at a gold mine in southern Oregon. That one, despite being no smaller and no less crazy to witness, had barely made the national papers—which was partly a product of the fact that it didn't have any wild-eyed charmers like LaVoy doing interviews at the front lines and partly, at least so far as I could figure it, because until the ferment of 2016 a wild standoff in the middle of nowhere had seemed too strange and random to mean much in a national sense. Now, just a few months later and a few counties over, the Malheur refuge looked like an expression of exactly where the country was headed.

But both of the earlier events, from Brandon's perspective, had gone well, and from a tactical standpoint there wasn't anything all that different about this one—except for a feeling of heaviness and foreboding that even Jason, who had been in on the plan since the beginning, seemed to share.

Brandon asked if he could call me back. The last time I'd seen him, six months earlier, I had encountered him by chance in his blue Dodge pickup on I-5 south of Eugene. We had convoyed through a rainstorm for an hour or so and then given each other a wave when we parted, the entire thing passing at seventy-five miles an hour without us exchanging a word, and we had a general sense that we could each trust the other. A few minutes later he called. "Listen, man," he said. "I've just been calling around. We have really good intel that the FBI is going to move in there tonight. And I'm wondering if you want to stay overnight with Jason, to be a sort of witness if some bad shit goes down."

This was only the first of many times over the next weeks and months that I'd be asked to put myself in a compromising position, and I realized only later how irretrievably compromised a position it was. In any case, I said yes, knowing that he was asking me to be, essentially, a human shield. I wandered over to the fire, where a few people were still getting the dozers in place to block the road. I asked if they really thought there'd be a raid. "That's the intel we got," one of them, a Mormon extremist and HVAC contractor from Las Vegas named

Brand Thornton, told me. "Our leaders briefed me on it. And the way I think it happens is we move this stuff up here"—he pointed to the dozers—"make a show of force, and I think they say to the superior officers, you know . . . I'm not sure this is such a good idea. . . . We have a lot more people here than you see."

We spoke for a minute about how many people were at the site, how little sleep they were getting, how everyone looked out for one another and loved one another. A thin young man in fatigues and a balaclava interjected, speaking so slowly that at first I thought he was stoned. "And we're good people," he said, nakedly baffled that the FBI had not chosen to see it this way. There was a long pause. "We're, like, the best people that you could possibly imagine."

CHAPTER 2

Our Government Is Completely Fucked

We loaded up into a government-owned F-250 diesel, manual transmission, that Jason had trouble getting into gear because of the AR-15 he'd jammed down next to the gearshift. It was January 5, 2016, and by then he'd spent almost a month in Harney County, a vast expanse of yellow-gray sagebrush basin interrupted rudely by a few basaltic uplifts colored with juniper and ponderosa in the higher elevations, an area almost the size of Massachusetts but counting only seven thousand residents. He had come, like many others, to participate in a countywide upheaval over the sentencing of two local ranchers—Dwight and Steven Hammond, father and son—over two illegal back-burns they'd allegedly set—either to keep approaching fires away from their property and to control noxious weeds, as they said, or to cover up evidence of poaching, as prosecutors said. The fires burned a few hundred acres of federal land. The ranchers, who'd had problems with the Bureau of Land Management and the management of the refuge for decades, had originally been sentenced to a year or less in prison, but federal antiterrorism law requires a minimum of a five-year sentence for any arson of federal property. This provision, somewhat ironically, was originally designed to target ecoterrorists. A federal judge refused to sentence the Hammonds to the statutory minimum, but after they were released the government managed to get the original sentence overturned on appeal, with the result that the two were being sent back to prison. Almost everyone in the county was outraged, and most of the county believed they had reason to be outraged at the federal government for reasons far bigger than the Hammonds.

On January 2, Ammon and Ryan Bundy had broken off from a protest in Burns and asked anyone who was willing to drive out and seize the empty collection of one-story sheds and offices that housed personnel at the refuge, a 187,000-acre, flat expanse of sagebrush desert centered around two so-called lakes, each a vast puddle with a muddy bottom and in most places only a few inches deep, that collected runoff from the mountains and supported in good years a large population of insects and tiny brine shrimp, which in turn were fed upon by migrating cranes, swans, and geese, and which the refuge now existed to protect. "It's time to take a hard stand," Ammon had said, standing on a snowbank in the parking lot of the Safeway in Burns, across the street from the Days Inn. His plans, which would take some time to become clear, were almost indescribably grandiose, and his motivations were so deeply spiritual that very few people outside his inner circle seem to have a handle on them even today.

Jason was one of only a few loyalists who followed Ammon to the refuge. And now they had made a curious pinprick on the American timeline: an armed pageant in which very little seemed to be at stake until things turned very grave, very quickly; a political protest that became world news without anyone managing to explain to the world what the whole thing was about; a standoff that was no larger or more aggressive than earlier militia actions in the West, but that came at a time when insurgency and political disintegration in this country had stopped seeming like the remote possibilities they had been in the years before. Suddenly, the young men with guns and tactical gear foretold of something disturbing—or hopeful, if you were of that state of mind—about the future of the country. Ammon and Ryan became famous to a degree that not even Ammon in his grandiosity could have anticipated, and there began a hysterical drive in the newspapers and by a sort of comical and pompous parade of supposed experts who followed the movement mostly by monitoring Facebook posts to analyze, categorize, and denounce it, feeding off one another until it seemed like eastern Oregon really was under some kind of mass assault.

I did not really think this was the case, though I did think something alarming and probably sinister had suddenly come to this corner of the world. But I'd spent much of the last few years bumbling around the West—sometimes reporting but mostly just drinking in smoky bars and living out of the back of a sturdy little Ford pickup—developing a sense that I'd found a society in the midst of a social breakdown. I'd fallen in love with the West a few years before, at the beginning of my twenties, less because I had any special idea of cowboy life or big landscapes and more because I was rootless, and because public lands afforded me a way to live basically for free on permanent vacation. I could load up the truck with nothing but a few cans of beer and beans and a few books about botany and geology, and drive out and live for free until I got bored or lonely, which rarely took long, and then I'd trundle on into some strange town and talk to girls and weird old miners and get drunk and make friends. As long as I could remember, I'd been of the persuasion shared by a kind of grouchy old enviro type who would be mostly happy to see the vast zone from the Pacific Coast to Colorado reconverted to wilderness and turned back as a paradise to Indians and anyone else who could confine themselves to using arrowheads and hafted axes to make a living. But in the meantime I found that I rather liked hanging out and getting into trouble with tough rancher ladies and outlaws and weathered miners, who, at least at their best, basically seemed to express a wildness just as enriching as you'd get alone out in the woods.

Over time I felt myself more at home there than I'd felt in any of the dozen or so places I bounced around to in my early twenties, trying to find a place to settle, and so I took on a very personal distress when I began to notice how much the place was dividing itself into irreconcilable camps. This was roughly along the political and cultural lines on which the whole country was dividing itself, and the process was driven by the same forces, but in the West the public lands—half the region's surface, a third of the country's—and the question of how they should be managed had become an easy test for where you stood in what was starting to feel like a civilizational conflict.

And even before the standoffs, when the issue was just the odd firebombing of a ranger station or sniper attack on Forest Service employee, the arguments were so personal and laden with the threat of violence that at first I simply wanted to understand what was going on. So I sought out militia guys and people on the angrier fringes of the rancher subculture. I wanted to document what I thought was an early slip in a national fault that was about to really come loose, and in part because I found it fascinating to watch an insurgency grow up on American soil, with mostly everyone outside the rural West totally unaware.

When the standoff at the Malheur (pronounced "Mal-yer" in this part of the world) refuge hit, I was living in New York, working a rather well-paid hustle as an investigator-for-hire for a guy who handled a lot of money. The job required little in terms of structured, day-to-day work, which had allowed me to sink into a drug-addled routine of wild drinking and manic dating. One of my uncles, whom I loved very much, had just died unexpectedly; and my grandmother, who was one of my best friends on earth, was on her own deathbed. It felt like my family was falling apart and, to be honest, when I read about the standoff, the whole thing seemed like a godsend—an easy adventure that might shape up into something of real historical significance and where at the very least I wouldn't spend all my nights bothering people for cocaine and talking to girls and avoiding calls from my mom about how much was too much to spend on hospice care for my grandmother or who should speak at my uncle's funeral. I found New York boring and wanted to be around guns and trucks and sagebrush again. At the beginning of 2016 it seemed enlivening to visit a place as it fell into actual armed chaos and rebellion, or at least it seemed preferable to following the impending national disaster online. I assumed—without bothering to make calls or confirm this for sure—that I'd know people at the refuge, and so I thought I'd go, talk my way into the place for a day or two, have a little adventure, write a short piece about it, and fly home. Paycheck.

The irony of this being that I didn't think I needed to be staying over with Jason, waiting for an FBI raid, to make my neat little plan for the week work, and I was annoyed that I'd already let myself get dragged in and to some degree implicated by an easy association with these guys. But it was exciting. We stopped off at a garage where the wildlife managers kept boats and heavy machinery. There was a giant backhoe, looking so shiny it seemed unlikely it had ever been used, and he caught me looking at it. "You want to drive the Cat?" he asked. I said that fuck yes I did. "You pay taxes, don't you?" he asked. "It belongs to you." I climbed up in the cab but realized that it would probably be crossing some kind of bounds of propriety to actually drive it around, so I left it. We headed over to the bunkhouse.

"I would have never thought, when we met," he said looking around and seeming almost as surprised as me, "that we would end up here eating pizza." It was an astonishingly comfortable building, with two long, leather couches arranged around a big-screen TV in a carpeted corner of the main room, a large, well-equipped kitchen area where we were standing, with a twenty-foot-long center island of sinks and counters laden with pizzas and homemade bread that some local women had dropped off earlier in the day. Down the corridor there were seven or eight small bedrooms with twin beds and cubbies, and a couple of bathrooms with satisfyingly hot water and good pressure in the showers. Everyone was out on guard still anticipating a raid that night. I asked about Jason's childhood, and he told me a story of growing up in rural Washington with a homesteading, Vietnam-vet father. "He bought five acres," he said, "and we cleared that land ourselves—Dad cut the trees, we burned out the stumps, he rented a dozer and leveled the ground, we poured a foundation. And so we lived in an eight-by-eight military tent for three months, a family of four, and then one day we moved to an eight-by-ten trailer, and we lived in that for a year and a half."

I took another piece of pizza and he went on. "So then one day that burned up because the space heater was too close to Dad's sock box, and we ended up getting a twenty-two-foot trailer, which me and my sister thought was like the fucking Taj Mahal. Then we got the house built—it wasn't completely finished but we got the occupancy permit—and we bought cows and chickens and rabbits and pigs. So I was like a rural farm boy, but not even a farm boy, because most people don't homestead themselves."

I was about to ask what had driven his dad to homestead when he cut me off. "And then my dad got cancer from Agent Orange, and I remember being eight years old and we were at the University of Washington and I was talking to the doctor and the doctor asked if I had any questions, and I said, 'Is it contagious?'

"And he said, 'No, it's not contagious.'

"And I said, 'Okay, well then, how did he get it?'

"And he said, 'Well, he got it in a war.' And so when I was twelve and the cancer came back, Dad said, 'Well, I can't do chemo again and go through all that, so I'm just going to ride it out,' and he died. And so I read everything I could about Agent Orange, and then I read everything I could about Vietnam, and then I read everything I could about the Constitution—and I realized: 'No standing armies'—I mean even the fact he was in the army was unconstitutional. I mean, our government is completely fucked."

He started working as a roofer when he was seventeen, and eventually he moved to Georgia, got married, started a business putting roofs on new houses during the housing boom, began work on a forty-eight-hundred-square-foot house of his own, and lost the business, the house, and the wife, after the crash. "And seeing the bailout?" he said. "I mean I was raging against the machine."

He recounted several arrests, one for drunken driving that he says was a setup, several for what he would describe as standing up for his rights to officers of the law, what others might regard as belligerence, and by the time he got to Harney County he had been charged with terroristic threats made toward a judge and a police officer and had lost his license.

"Now they've got me in maximum security," he said, talking about the last arrest, "with ankle chains and belly chains, they don't let me call anybody for four days, nobody even knows I'm in jail. And I'm like, 'Dude—this is America, you've got me in here like a Nazi, just push the gas button.' And finally a guy comes to me and says you're charged with terroristic threats, you threatened an officer and a judge. They give me bond, I'm not supposed to leave the state of Georgia, I'm not supposed to be near firearms." He laughed. "But meanwhile, I'm standing here in Oregon, taking a federal building," he said. "I don't quit. I'm like the Energizer bunny of the Constitution."

We were still the only people in the bunkhouse, and maybe the only people on the refuge, who hadn't been consumed by the paranoia of the night. Sean and Sandy Anderson, a couple in their forties with matching camo getups, matching deer rifles, and matching far-north Wisconsin accents, came up, deeply freaked out and claiming to have seen figures moving at the rear gate entrance to the compound, which they'd been guarding. Their radio wasn't working. Jason tried his. It wouldn't work either. We never did figure out whether they'd been jammed. They asked about drones. Jason remained resolutely unbothered. He asked if I wanted to go meet Ammon.

We drove over, left the truck idling outside, and tried the door of the stone office. It was locked. We didn't know it at the time, but the mood inside the office was such that Ammon's bodyguard raised his AR-15 and pointed it toward the door, ready to fire through the tongue-and-groove boards if the knob rattled again. Jason went for the knob and took it in his hand, then paused. "I guess they're busy," he said, and we turned back toward the truck. Inside, with the lights off and at least one gun set to fire through a closed door, with every reason to believe that federal agents had come for him in a night raid, Ammon Bundy leaned back in a swivel chair and played with his iPhone. "Oh," he said, to no one in particular, "it's fun to live this way."

CHAPTER 3

Landscape of Rebellion I

The Great Basin, where most of this story takes place, is an endorheic drainage basin. This is to say that it's a contiguous set of landscapes with no freshwater outlet to the sea. Most of the Southwest is drained by the Colorado River, which means that if you spit into a little mountain stream anywhere in the state of Arizona, it should run downhill and find, maybe, a creek feeding into a branch of the Gila, which would join the main stem and then the Colorado and then run your DNA all the way into the Sea of Cortez—or at least it would have before dams and irrigation takings made it so that the Colorado now almost never reaches the sea. A lot of the Northwest is drained by the Columbia. Most of California and even parts of Oregon are drained by less famous rivers, carrying snowmelt from the Cascades, the Sierra Nevada, the Siskiyous, and other ranges west toward the Pacific. These mountains, which form a more or less contiguous north-south wall from Mexico to the Canadian border, cause water-bearing clouds from the west to shed their moisture as they rise, producing great snowpacks in the Sierra Nevada and the Cascades. They effectively form a sort of secondary continental divide, where rivers flow westward down the relatively lush slope of the Sierra through oak woodlands and on to the Pacific, while on the eastern slope the remaining moisture falls as snow on the high peaks then trickles into the Great Basin, which runs from the California desert east to Wyoming, and from Arizona up all the way to Oregon. Harney County is located in the very northernmost extent of the Great Basin, and when you drive north of Burns there's a roadside marker miles outside of town, leaning a bit on its post across from a dingy clapboard gift shop run by a very lonely-seeming mother and her teenage daughter, indicating where the basin stops and the Columbia River drainage begins.

The Great Basin sweeps across the West, assembled out of rings of mountains where water runs off and pools in anything from a marshy flat to an inland sea. To some degree it's only geological happenstance that so many of the puzzle pieces have fitted together to form the greater basin, but this is the drainage pattern that made the Bonneville Salt Flats, the Great Salt Lake, Mono Lake in California, and the muddy lakes of the Malheur National Wildlife Refuge.

Then things get confusing, because there are lots of ways of drawing boundaries around the Great Basin that don't exactly have to do with hydrology. There's a Great Basin desert, which gives its name to the northern portion of the huge, contiguous interior American desert, even though technically the basin itself dips southward like a peninsula into parts of the Mojave. Some books talk about a Great Basin Floristic Province, and there's a simple sort of layman's shorthand for the floristic province—which is just to say that the Great Basin is anywhere the basin sagebrush grows dominant. And then

there's a sort of Great Basin state of mind, which would probably exclude all of the basin parts of California but would
extend the bounds east, into the Colorado River drainages
of eastern Utah and northern Arizona, and north, into the
Snake and Columbia drainages of southern Idaho, eastern
Oregon, and western parts of Colorado, Wyoming, and even
Montana.

These places have something in common that goes far
beyond simply being *western*. They're history obsessed, and
their major poles of political power are really just modern
updates on the forces that drove settlement in the first place—
the mining, oil, and gas industries, ranchers, and the Mormon Church—and the culture looks inward in a way that
uncannily matches the hydrology of the region. There's an
endearing everybody-knows-everybody feel, especially among
Mormons, ranchers, and Mormon ranchers. "I just saw Hank
Jones," someone'll say, and somebody else will say, "Was that
the Hank Jones up in Nevada or the one that used to have the
trucking company over in Arizona?" And then whichever
Hank it was, somebody'll ask how his kids are and the conversation will go from there. Ten-hour drives to visit a friend
aren't much of an event. Nowadays distant neighbors—young
and also very old—keep in touch on Facebook and maintain
vicious public feuds and argue about insane conspiracy theories and post heartfelt remembrances of dead aunts with an
energy that makes twentysomething New Yorkers on Snapchat
look sedate. The first white settlers of the area were mostly Mormons, who brought with them an intense suspicion of federal
authority, and the bounds of this state of mind still conform

more or less to the lines of the original state of Deseret that Brigham Young proposed to carve into Zion, before the federal government blocked him. Most of the settlers who came after them were only passing through on the way to California and Oregon, and the non-Mormons who stayed did so because they liked the space and thought themselves tough enough to make a life logging, mining, or ranching in country that even the most hard-ass homesteaders found too rough to want to claim. This has given people even today a sense of inherited pride and purchase on the lands in the region, all of which were opened after the Mexican-American War and the conquest of the Indians to the unreserved public domain. Most of these lands were never claimed, not just because nobody wanted to claim waterless desert, but because there wasn't any real need to claim them—in the days of the open range you could run cattle, mine, log, and more or less take what you could get from the land without filling out much paperwork or answering to anyone as to whether it was a good idea to clear-cut that whole hillside or not. The lands, stolen fair and square by an army paid for by the whole country, still functionally belonged to the westerners who used them and who depended on them, literally, for their survival.

This worked out pretty well for a while—at least for everyone but the Indians, trees, waterways, bison, and bothersome predators who the ranchers quickly set out to extirpate. Now, among people who see themselves as descendants of a certain way of life, there exists a shared memory of a golden era between the end of the Indian wars and the closing of the frontier, when men were men and you could claim a homestead and run your cattle how you saw best, without an army of bureaucrats staring down from Washington concocting formulas to tell you how many head the mountain valley your family might have been grazing on for three generations could support. Free people were good stewards of the land by definition, because they owed a debt to their neighbors and their children to keep the range in good condition and to pass it on down to their posterity. In this telling, the Great Basin became a sort of cradle for an idealized version of a free American life. The problems came when the rest of the country stopped believing this story, and when they decided they wanted to manage the unclaimed lands in the national interest, for their own children. Then things began to go crazy.

CHAPTER 4

The Tip of the Spear

I spent that night in Jason's room. We had a long argument about who would take the bed, each of us insisting that we were fine on the floor. He won, but it ended up being immaterial. We came back, still unaware of what had happened behind Ammon's barricaded door, and spent a couple of hours hanging in the bunkhouse with people who had filtered in as things seemed to calm down outside. There was a young brown-haired logger, from somewhere in far northern California, who had a much older girlfriend he kept making out with while we sat around the big island in the kitchen. There were several older guys who made a big faux-military to-do about not wanting to give their names, not that I cared beyond asking out of politeness or thought that it would help them much in the end. One of them has already taken a plea deal. But they were friendly enough after a minute of briefing Jason on the state of the siege as they saw it. Everyone slowly got out of their tactical gear and hats and gloves and put their long guns off to the side and adjusted their holsters—very few of them seemed much used to carrying openly at this point—and soon we had all relaxed. It seemed absurd that no one had a beer open, but it would be weeks before the rules on substance use relaxed. This was at the very start of the standoff—two days after it began—and already someone had thought to place an earnest little handwritten sign outside the bunkhouse reading "No Cigs on the Ground, No Chew on the Ground." Jason fell asleep on one of the leather couches while everyone was still talking. He looked pretty happy, so the rest of them went to bed, and I let him snore while I brewed a foul-tasting opiate tea that I'd brought as a higher-intensity backup because I didn't want to miss a day of the standoff if I got busted with pot on the plane. It made me feel more nauseous and disoriented than sleepy, but luckily there was a door that led straight outside from our little room in the bunk, and I stayed up in just my long underwear and cowboy boots, leaning on the doorjamb smoking cigarettes, getting higher and higher off more tea, reading the same three pages of a Doris Lessing story, and thinking that if a sentry came by and saw me it would be a real task to explain who I was and what I was doing. Jason came in just as I'd finally laid down to sleep. I pretended to be out already and he leaned his AR against the wall, unclipped the holster holding his .45, and stuck it with the keys and change from his pocket in a cubbyhole above my head. He then lay down, without removing his belt or shoes, belly-down on the hard floor, without so much as improvising a pillow from a spare shirt. He fell asleep almost instantly and was right there snoring when I woke with the daylight. I still find this impressive.

I had coffee and a banana in the kitchen with Joe and Jason, and then left them to go wander around. It felt very nice to be there. The sun had come out and the temperature had risen to above freezing. The gray-green of the sagebrush against patches of yellow grit of the desert pavement and the blue of the sky and the dark of the little volcanic cinder cones poking out of the desert floor and the looming, ponderosa-and-juniper-shrouded mountains that ringed the basin struck you at once—in that particularly western way where it doesn't serve to spend too much time dwelling on the scale and beauty of the place or you'll be overwhelmed. From the small rise where I'd parked and where the fire tower stood, there was really nothing to obstruct your view across the floor of the basin to Steens Mountain, a meandering fifty-mile-long basalt spine, lushly purple and fringed like a king's robe with a band of snow at the top. The day was absurdly clear. It looked like it couldn't be more than an hour's hike to the base of the mountain. It was forty-five miles away.

I wandered back toward the car. Ammon had just finished his daily morning press conference, or at least I think he had, because cable news cameramen and grunt-level militiamen in their stock getups of camo, boots, and balaclavas were milling around, each watching the other with obvious disdain, each knowing that the other was the only justification for their presence there. The Bundys had given reporters, locals, and really anyone who wanted to come more or less free passage about the place during daylight hours—this was their way of showing that they'd returned the land to the people and also a way of drawing attention and building support—and journalists could wander around, writing stories without needing to pull any of the leaders aside for solo access, and curious locals were encouraged to wander around and talk to Ammon and Ryan personally, which gave the brothers a chance to expound their philosophy and indoctrinate the willing. These meetings took place in the little stone office that Ammon had commandeered as his own. Journalists and most occupiers were generally barred from the place, but local ranchers were welcome to walk right in.

The FBI remained unseen, aside from a small plane making occasional overflights, and all the guns and security at the perimeter were in preparation for a surprise assault. This was fun too, in a dark way. I was a kid in the '90s, when we grew up under the impression that the world had settled into a static, end-of-history kind of order, and many of us were still too young when 9/11 happened to think it had changed the paradigm all that much. It had been maybe my dearest wish, as a teenager, that something would upend things. In my early twenties, I developed an opposite terror that we had already made a rent in the national fabric so deep that eventually there would have to be some sort of cataclysm. This was a feeling I formed mostly by hanging out in bars in the darker and stranger pockets of the South and the West, so it was a little hard to express persuasively. But now it seemed very clear. The country was going insane, and at least here you could see the mechanisms at work. I lit a cigarette and spoke for a while to an old guy in Carhartts I knew by sight but who didn't want to give his name. "It's the amalgamation and agglomeration of events," he said. "That's what got them paying attention finally. Just wait till Hillary gets in there. This right here is just the tip of the spear."

That night the sheriff was hosting a community meeting, at the fairgrounds in Burns. I drove up to town, expecting to stop in with a few people sitting around tables in a community center, and found myself stuck in what might have been the only traffic jam in the history of Harney County. It took me half an hour to get to the fairgrounds from the traffic light at the center of town. The fairground lot was full, and parked cars were lined up along the road for at least half a mile in either direction. Hundreds upon hundreds of people, the women done up against the cold, the men mostly in full buckles-hats-boots rancher dress-up regalia, had turned out. It was more than the garage-like hall could hold, and so they threw open the roll-up doors so the people standing outside in the freezing lot could watch. It was cold, flashbulbs were going off constantly, the atmosphere crackling.

A pastor got up to open the meeting with a prayer and then the sheriff, a florid and earnest forty-something former army medic and drill sergeant named David Ward, who was only just finishing his first year on the job, stood up. He gave a long and affecting speech about his military service and about how much he loved the county. He directed much of it at Ammon. He asked him to "go home and let us get back to our lives in Harney County," which provoked a long standing ovation. It was all moving—the prayer, the tearful speech verging on a plea, the hundreds of people. "At this point nobody's been hurt," he went on. "There's some things going on in the community— maybe it was our visitors, maybe it wasn't—with deputies followed home, their families followed around. Somebody flattened my wife's tire recently. She packed up and left town. The stress was too much. Somebody from out of town came and followed my parents around." He had his parents stand and they got an ovation. "I too have concerns about the direction this country is headed," he went on. "But I intend to handle those by talking to my friends and neighbors and organizing movements and taking this country back at the ballot box." He talked for a long time, was in tears through a lot of it, and kept getting interrupted by applause. But the message of his speech was somewhat different than what he'd been telling the out-of-town press, which was that Harney County stood united against the occupation. "I know those folks," he said, talking about the Hammonds, "and I've got my own opinions about what happened, but we don't solve this through armed rebellion.

"There's been people in the community that's been involved on one side or the other," he went on. "But this is America—we get to disagree with each other without violence or threats of retribution. There's people in this room I disagree with wholeheartedly, and you don't get to threaten me, because I'm an American." This produced some halting applause. "So I'm here to ask, whatever side of the fence we're on here in Harney County, that we mend those fences, put on a united front, and ask those folks out at the refuge to pick up and go home." The crowd was quite still. "And we're going to work on the problems that we face here in Harney County ourselves." There was a modest cheer. And then he began to lose the narrative. He asked how many people in the crowd were from Harney County. Most people raised their hands. Then he asked, "How many people want to work this out peacefully"—an ovation began to rise at this—"and ask these folks to go home." The ovation half-stopped and suddenly a competing chorus of "No!" rose up. Someone in the back yelled, "Let 'em stay!" People began clapping to *that*.

It turned out that the people cheering for the sheriff couldn't have been much more than half the crowd, and things quickly turned darker and more complicated than the visitors had been expecting. Ward opened the floor. The second speaker, a tall, young, and impossibly clean-cut rancher in hat and boots, came up and began reading with endearing awkwardness from a prepared statement. He talked about his wife, who he said taught in the county and was upset about the schools being closed. But then he changed direction. "That being said, I appreciate much of their methods," he said, referring to the Bundys, "and admire their sense of doing the right thing." He said he'd been down to visit them and had found them friendly and open to dialogue. "Whether you agree or disagree with Bundy's movement," he said, reading awkwardly, like a kid at a middle school graduation, "he has given Harney County our biggest and best platform to get our message out." The crowd gave its first pro-Bundy ovation. There would be many more to come.

The "message" he was talking about was a layered thing, and it was lost on most of the national reporters who came to the meeting—who more or less wrote it up according to the official line, as a heartwarming stand by Good Simple People against armed politics and division and other bad stuff like that.

Part of it was topical. Almost everyone in the county thought the Hammonds had been treated brutally, and the speakers kept circling back to issues that never really made it into the papers—fears that the Obama administration would designate a portion of BLM land in neighboring Malheur County as a national monument, fears that the sage grouse would get listed as an endangered species, anger over reductions in logging and in allowed animal unit months, which is bureaucracy-speak for how many cows or sheep a rancher can run on public ground. When speaking of cattle, an AUM is one cow-calf pair, for sheep it's five animals. All these are decisions made by land managers and federal officials, done in theory for the collective good—but the collective's interest in these lands has expanded greatly in the last few decades, and with it there's been a corresponding change in what good land management for the public interest looks like. Federal courts and basic common sense would say that a rancher's permits allowing her to graze her animals on public land aren't *property*, in the sense that a truck I buy at a dealership is my property. The permits are a privilege, granted by the federal government in the name of the American people.

This seems simple enough in the East, where grass and water are easy to come by and you can raise a lot of animals on a pretty small patch of ground. But in the dry vastnesses of the West, you need to be able to run cows on thousands and thousands of acres to support a midsize ranch. Most people can't afford to buy a spread like this, so for as long as there have been federal grazing permits ranches that abut federal land have been bought and sold with the value of those permits built into the value of the property. I happen to believe that cows never should have been sent out to look for food in the western deserts in the first place. But now if the federal government picks a patch of ground, say by creating a new national monument, and then cuts back grazing in the name of preserving a beautiful wild space, the new designation not only risks making it impossible for a rancher to run enough cows to break even—it also can end up taking a property that he spent his life savings on, and which might be the only thing of value he has to pass on to his kids, and leave it functionally worthless.

An unspoken undercurrent to the meeting was that a lot of people in Harney County think that this is exactly how the Malheur refuge grew—that they established a refuge and cut grazing on it, which reduced the value of the adjoining ranches, which forced the ranchers to sell out, which grew the refuge.

Then on to take the next neighbor's ranch, and so on. And they think that the Hammonds were singled out for what by any measure seems like a harsh charge, bearing a bizarrely heavy sentence, because they "stood up to the BLM."

This is the phrase you hear over and over, and not just from the ranchers out in the remoter fringes of the county, of whom a pretty good percentage were receptive to anything Ammon wanted to say. I passed through Burns a full year and a half after the standoff and spent a few hours over an early breakfast with Fran Davis, who runs the little deli on Broadway and a bed-and-breakfast that's well worth a visit if you're making a hunting trip to the area. "It just breaks my heart that I can't send you up the road to meet Dwight Hammond right now," she said. "And when it's all over and they're out of prison—which, for us, is when this will really be all over—you'll have to come back here and I'll introduce you. He is just a very fine man, and you can see right here that I pay my bills and work at this deli that barely breaks even and I don't try to get into any of all that business. But I ranch here too, and for us Dwight was always who said what it was that we wouldn't say to all them, and they punished him for it."

By "all them" she meant the BLM and refuge managers. "There are many that are good," she said, and by example she referenced Bill, the owner of the Pine Room bar over by the Days Inn, who had just retired from the BLM after decades of work. "But I remember when they started with the Hammonds—my son was over at the place, twelve years old, and they went over and were going to put a fence around their water gap," which is to say that they were going to block off the Hammonds' door to access a fenced-off wetland in the refuge. Riparian areas and wetlands in the West are often blocked off to protect them from the damage cattle cause, and in the desert a water gap can be a rancher's only way of keeping a herd alive.

"And they didn't take anyone else's water gap that year, but they were going to put a fence around Dwight's, and so he went and stood by it to try to stop them, because he didn't have any other way to water his cattle. And they arrested him right in front of my twelve-year-old son. And I just thought—I mean what else could you think?—they were out to get him. And he's one of the best people you will ever meet. But stubborn." Refuge officials at the time filed affidavits claiming that Hammond had been threatening them for years, reportedly telling one that he was going to "tear his head off and shit down his neck." Still, five hundred ranchers showed up the next week to protest the arrests. This was two decades ago.

Small-time miners and loggers have their own versions of these problems, which are made more intractable by the fact that somebody has to be in charge of enforcing restrictions on land use, which, today, are generally pushed by environmentalists and decided on by officials working for Washington-based agencies. Those people are the range techs and forest rangers of the BLM and the Forest Service, and they're dealing with communities where some large percentage of people don't want them there, don't agree with the rules they're enforcing, where people have gotten progressively poorer over the last few decades, and have lots of guns. I always try to tell angry westerners that they could not possibly imagine how much harder they'd have it dealing with the police in most any black neighborhood in this country. I tell them that the resources they'd love to maintain the same access to that they'd always had are now increasingly desired by others, and that there's going to have to be some give on their part. But this is a hard argument to make, because the sympathetic figures of angry ranchers have been manipulated very successfully by a network of oligarchical billionaires and major companies—resource conglomerates with an interest in breaking down drilling and mining restrictions; or donor idealogues who use the image of beset ranchers facing off against the big bad feds to try to color all environmental regulation and any attempt to address the issue of climate change as tyrannous federal overreach. These groups have quietly funded a push by western politicians and think tanks to give public lands over to the states, which they are fully aware would have a very hard time paying to maintain the lands. Many of these states are run by politicians who are resolutely opposed to even the barest environmental protections, and who are lavishly funded by the same groups pushing the idea of privatization or state transfer. There's no reason to doubt that the transferred lands would quickly be parceled off to mining and gas interests for uses far more destructive than ranching, developers, and rich guys looking for private hunting grounds. It's hard to imagine ranchers liking this outcome very much.

But still a lot of rural people across the Great Basin have come to feel like an occupied minority, and every once in a while today you'll see a Ranchers' Lives Matter sign at a protest or tacked to a fencepost, in case the point wasn't clear. It's this feeling of impotence in the face of an alien occupation that had people so worked up about the Hammonds being sent back to prison. And it's this anger that Ammon was able to use.

Things went back and forth for about an hour, until a bearded young silversmith named Pat Horlacher, who would have looked more at home in Seattle than out here in the desert, came up and described how many ranchers in the area would have liked to have gone out and talked to the Bundys but didn't "for one simple reason: they were afraid of the BLM and the repercussions that would happen if they did." This produced a very long cheer. "That you could lose your permits by simply going down and talking to these people," he went on. "These are pillars in this community, these are big outfits—and they're scared of the BLM! When did that happen?"

The crowd erupted. "I hear these ideas of working through an appropriate channel—and I have yet to hear any time we have worked through an 'appropriate channel' that actually worked!"

As far as the sheriff's hopes for the night went, this was the end. As far as most of the reporters assembled saw it, the story of the night had ended a long time ago, and they wrote the official line. I found this baffling. I think it wasn't conceivable to most of them that this collection of Good Simple People was seriously conflicted about whether or not to embrace the insurrection in their midst, and so they reported what their experience told them was plausible—just like you might hopefully assume the footsteps in the night were the cat acting funny, or just as you might assume the people at the meeting would never vote in a lying used-car salesman as president of the United States.

CHAPTER 5

The Sunset Route

I came to the rural West by hitchhiking. I was twenty, and I'd dropped out of college in Montreal, where I'd chosen to go more or less at random, because it seemed as different as possible from where I'd grown up, in Cincinnati. It didn't suit me for a lot of reasons, but the easiest to articulate was that being in Quebec, where the bars are full of people who've known one another since high school and whose families have been intertwined and rooted on the cold rolling expanse of the Canadian shield for centuries, made me homesick for the United States. I found I envied their sense of belonging, the way the culture and the landscape seemed to blend so cleanly—the opening line of Quebec's great national song translates roughly to "My country, it's not a country, it's winter"—and even their politics. Quebec is full of wild, rough people, and plenty of them own guns, but still lots of Quebecois who here would be called rednecks vote for proudly left-wing parties—which I thought was cool, even though I was a teenage anarchist and thought of voting in the United States as a sham exercise to cover up the fact that a few rich people controlled our politics. I didn't exactly stop thinking that, but I did find that I wanted to confront and try to get over my alienation from politics in America and, more diffusely, an alienation from my family and from the culture in which I'd grown up. And so I wandered around the Northeast, aimlessly working handyman jobs, went back to Cincinnati for a while, and then took off to ride freight trains and hitchhike west.

This was at the tail end of a long and tentative rapprochement between me and my maternal grandmother, whom I called Jen—because none of us grandchildren had been able to pronounce her name, Jean, and because she refused to be called Grandma—and who had always been the dominant emotional and cultural figure in our family. In time we became great friends and she grew into one of my closest confidantes, but as I was growing up it had always been very clear to me that she tended to view me and my immediate family with a skeptical eye, which I bitterly resented, and which had contributed to a reflexive disdain bordering on loathing that I developed for the cultural milieu of southwestern Ohio. She was a firm upholder of the values and pretensions to aristocracy shared by a certain sort of resident of Cincinnati's East Side, which, for white people, was a clubby place marked by brass-button blazers and ladies' bridge games, where kids went to a small set of private schools and tended to stick around, going to in-state universities, and marrying one another young.

My mom, unlike her two brothers and unlike almost anyone she grew up with, went off to college and jumped headfirst into the cultural revolutions of the sixties, which eventually led to her coming back and marrying my dad, a soft-spoken country boy from central Ohio, who was then in a very intense

Leninist working group and who had three daughters from an earlier marriage. He had always been poor and had raised my sisters in Section 8 housing—in a neighborhood where at that time, in a disintegrating city, few white people even dared to visit, much less live. I spent the first eleven years of my life just up the hill, in a neighborhood with dope boys on the corner and where I didn't think to find it strange that I was the only white kid in the nightly pickup baseball games we played in the cul-de-sac down the street. But we eventually moved out east, to the near-rural fringes of the city, which I found disorienting and lonely at first, because I couldn't figure a way to get on with the jocky Catholic-school boys in the neighborhood, and which only exacerbated for me the feeling of alienation from my grandmother and my cousins, who seemed to fit so easily into the world of the East Side.

But I came to love it, because we had five hundred acres of woods behind our house. We didn't own any of the land, but you could follow deer trails back for miles without ever seeing a soul, because most of it was owned by a rich family down the road, for whom the woods served as a buffer surrounding a cluster of mansions they reached by driving down a winding half-mile private drive. I hit the woods every day after school, just to wander and play make-believe. At first it didn't occur to me that anyone would care I was back there, and when the grumpy old men who lived in the mansions began to spot me from their cars as they drove the private road, and then to at first yell at me and then to call the cops and finally to physically threaten me, I took it as a basically military challenge, which I met with extravagant defiance. I developed a pack of friends who ran in the woods with me, and we grew into a tribe of feral little outlaws, leaving notes on the road to show our omnipresence, letting ourselves get seen by the grumpy old men and daring them to call the cops on us, knowing that in those woods I could guide us down trails and over hills and out of the reach of any pursuit. We became expert shoplifters, and hid our caches in the woods, and we even once robbed the cache of a local drug dealer, who'd hidden a stolen moped in a gully. We wheeled it home, fixed it up, and sold it.

They were my woods—I looked after them and knew every trail and gully better than anyone else ever would, and I learned at a very young age what a delicious and irreplaceable gift it can be to have a place to roam and think and be with yourself in the secure knowledge that you won't meet anyone, that no one can intrude to see you acting a fool and pretending to cut down armies with a stick as a sword, or to overhear your muttering as you plan out how to talk to a pretty girl. I became addicted to the feel of them, the braided experience of connection to nature, privacy, and unpoliceable freedom—and, to fast-forward a bit, this is the feeling that made me fall in love with public lands in the West, after spending years in the East visiting parks and finding them crowded and full of rules and generally underwhelming. And it's why—as much as I have a near religious obsession with trying to find a way for people to live on this earth without fucking it up more than they already have—I'm a bit skeptical of the idea that tossing out regulations and walling off preserved spaces is the only way to deal with public land. Wilderness is only really wild if you can be wild on it.

I eventually cooled off a bit, after getting arrested a couple of times for shoplifting and vandalism—though not over anything that happened in my woods, which I still tend to think of as offering a kind of druidic protection circle—and I took my delinquent energies and threw them into shoplifting books about politics. This was around the time of the 2000 election, when the moderately right-wing consensus that had defined the politics of the area for so long devolved into a bitter and very personal set of divisions. This has happened everywhere now, but it was especially raw in southwestern Ohio, which was growing into the swingiest portion of America's great swing state, and where it was very easy, and true, to think that the fate of the country hung on just a few votes. The stodgy order of my grandmother's East Side dissolved in those years, and I watched as many of the middle-class white men—the fathers of my friends who'd been its firmest upholders—fell into debt and divorce, drunkenness and early decrepitude. In 2001 we had a major riot, after a long series of police killings of unarmed black men, which shattered the inner neighborhoods where my sisters and I had grown up and ignited for lots of white males a combination of frantic paranoia and dreamy fantasies of race wars in which they'd crack open their gun safes and stride out to defend their families against the onrushing hordes. It began to feel like we lived on the front lines of the war that was opening between our two great politico-cultural tribes. The men in our neighborhood loved the rhetoric of the Bush campaigns—especially in 2004, when you were either with us or against us, when Republicans were running ads like the one calling Howard Dean a "tax-hiking, government-expanding, latte-drinking, sushi-eating, Volvo-driving, *New York Times*–reading, body-piercing, Hollywood-loving, left-wing freak show." I'm sure I'm not the only person to have grown up in those years, in a place like Ohio, who took words like that very personally—an attack on the basic sense that people like the members of my family were Real Americans, which became a phrase I heard all the time, an unsubtle dagger wielded by guys talking politics to my dad at cookouts, or shouted from the windows of a pickup truck at me because he had stuck a John Kerry sticker on the bumper of the car I drove to school. This was only the beginning. By the time of the 2016 election things were so heated that a neighbor dropped by to talk to my mom, correctly assuming she didn't have any guns in the house. He said he respected her bravery in putting up a Hillary sign. "I wanted to let you know," he said, "that if things get ugly I'll be here to help."

This was all meant to be taken very personally—it was politics acting as sorting mechanism for white people, to harden a tribal allegiance to right-wing politics based on a sense of shared cultural markers, and to challenge the basic patriotism of anyone who didn't get in line. I responded to it with a combination of hot rage and the lonely unmoored feeling of a teenager trying and failing to find a culture to grow into.

I began to grow close with Jen, my uncle Reppie—my mom's older brother—and my cousins, who all seemed to represent a world with a cultural order and continuity that I found attractive, even if I never figured out a way to really be a part of it. And those years let Jen resign herself to the way I was. She saw that her social order was collapsing, and she'd been through years of fighting and judging my mother for failing to uphold it. She decided not to repeat this with me—which as a teenager I found shocking and hard to trust, even as I went to her house for dinner every Tuesday with my cousins and slowly began to tell her about my problems with girls and hopes for the future. But she was wild herself. She'd been a pilot during World War II, ferrying bombers, which is something she later got a Congressional Gold Medal for, handed out by our own Cincinnati boy John Boehner. She had run away to the Bahamas to be the secretary for an expatriate aristocrat, who'd fallen in love with her and locked her in his château until she escaped and fled to the American embassy. She had worked for the symphony in Cincinnati, and had been friendly with Arthur Rubinstein and John Updike and had entertained and kept up with Glenn Gould on wild pill benders. She, alone among everyone in our family, saw herself in me at the moment I dropped out of college, and she was the only one who I really felt comfortable confiding to, in the months when it had become my abiding obsession to see every part of the country, to know its strangest corners and wildest people and to be able to use that intimacy as a club against anyone who wanted to challenge my sense of belonging or the idea that growing up left-wing is somehow incompatible with patriotism or a true connection to whatever constitutes the deepest strands of Americana. I was grateful beyond words to her that she didn't challenge that project, or think it silly and grandiose.

Reppie—so called because of his initials, Robert Elliott Pogue—died of a sudden heart attack just a couple of days before Christmas 2015, and just a couple of weeks before I went to Oregon. It was also on the night of the birthday he shared with Jen, which we as a family had internalized as a symbol of the special and almost unaccountable closeness they'd always had. Jen, ninety-five years old and lying on her deathbed with a basketball-size tumor growing in her stomach, was still lucid enough to take in the enormity of the situation, and to be fully devastated. She had clung so doggedly to life, for so long, and her reward was to be stuck in bed, hearing from my mom and little cousin that she'd outlasted her son. She just stared when my mom told her, unable to form words and almost gasping. But by the time I got back to Cincinnati later that week, Reppie's death seemed to have almost given her a new fight, and she was sitting up and lucid when I came to her. I saw her every day for a week, passing the time talking about Rep and books and my love life. I took off back to New York for a few days, and then Ammon took over the refuge. This was the last time I saw her.

So when I went, it felt like I was losing my family mooring—my two great connections to a social order that I'd now never really have a chance or reason to grow into, even if it was still very hard to picture myself going to prim cocktail parties or waiting for the kids to spill out of Sunday school, under the redbuds and beeches of our southern Ohio. And I think that part of what seemed nice about going to the refuge was that it offered at least a sense of coherence and direction in my own life, if only because it felt a bit like a continuation of my long-ago project when I came back to Cincinnati and then hoboed west.

That fall, eight years earlier, I caught a freight train out of Cincinnati, spent a couple of weeks in Atlanta and Louisiana with a trucker headed for Texas, and got wrapped up in some things on the way that left me much more grown by the time I hit Beaumont than when I'd left.

I spent a cold night trying to beg a westbound ride outside a truck stop, and at dawn I finally caught out with a wiry old trucker from somewhere in Trans-Pecos Texas. He wore a big brown hat and drove trucks only as a side job. His main business was a ranch he kept, which had, when he'd bought it, supported cattle. He had mostly abandoned this as unprofitable. "Cattle die for a living" was a memorable thing he said about that. "You also have to pay Mexicans to babysit them." He had expanded his leases, and over slow decades of growth he had switched over to a low-profit but low-cost business selling mesquite logs for firewood and chips for barbecue. He had steady clients and restaurants, but he also kept up a farm stand near his place, which, when he was in town, he manned himself. "I like to meet people, and I like cash for tax purposes," he said. He showed me a printed photograph of himself in full cowboy regalia—by the stand, the white-yellow rock and creosote bush of the Chihuahuan Desert in the background. He was holding what was very recognizably a 1911 model .45 semiautomatic. "You see the gun?" he asked. I said it was hard to miss. "I took that photo for the police," he said. I didn't have to encourage him to go on. "Not the first time one of 'em tried to rob me, but it was the first time I shot one."

"One what?"

"Oh man, you know." He meant a Mexican. "He comes up to me in a Thunderbird, you know, like one of those cars that the boys who think they're real tough drive. So I was already kinda looking out. And he comes up shifty. He speaks good English but he's asking about firewood in a way that kinda tells me he doesn't burn a lot of firewood, and I can see he's looking for the cash box. So I'm following his eyes and then I look down and he's got a fillet knife in his right hand, like out of a movie, you know? Like a thief in Old Mexico with a stiletto! I was almost impressed. But I just took out the pistol and told him to step on back. He just kinda stood there, and so I said that if that's how he was going to be, where did he want it? He just looked at me. I said, 'Where do you want it?' He kept on looking, and so I shot him in the thigh. Then he got the message and took off."

It only later occurred to me to wonder how the wounded fellow had managed to take off after getting shot in the thigh with a big .45 round, but who really knows. "That's when I formed a group to try to prevent this sort of thing." This was just shortly after the Minuteman militias had just been making news. I asked if it was part of that. "Not part of it but something like it. We're more just old cowboys, where those guys are more like, you know, black helicopters and stuff like that. But the way this world is going, those black helicopter people may turn out to be right." He showed me a picture of him and about a dozen or so other guys in the militia arrayed in a semicircle, on horseback, just like an old posse. I can't remember what I said about this.

It was only several years later, hitchhiking and passing by a bar hard by the interstate in Waco called Papa Joe's, that I heard about a case that had been very famous in Texas from the year I'd ridden out with the trucker. The country singer Billy Joe Shaver, one of my favorites, had been drinking at Papa Joe's and had had words with a man named Billy Bryant Coker, who followed him out into the parking lot. It was alleged—though Billy Joe was eventually acquitted on grounds of self-defense—that Billy Joe pulled a gun out of his truck and asked, "Where do you want it?" When he supposedly didn't get a response, he shot him in the face. This shooting took place in April 2007, just a few months before I caught a ride with this supposed militia-cowboy trucker. It would seem to be giving a lot of benefit of the doubt to think he hadn't heard about it and stolen the quote. It was around this time I began to notice how much of what seems to be deep American authenticity is really just pageantry.

CHAPTER 6

A First Summer in the Sierra

Four years later, I was sitting at the bar at the Zane Iron Horse Lounge, in Sonora, California. I was with friends, insomuch as travelers who drink late and stay for a couple of weeks can come to know everyone in a small-town bar, and I was specifically with two brothers. They were in their thirties, ran some sort of logistics business, which was why they were in town, and were both very intense in very different ways. We had several big nights at the bar, all sparked by the energies of Bill, the older one, who was dark-haired and clean-shaven and jovial and claimed to have been in prison on a Level III yard. "I wasn't the white shot caller," he said the night I met him, which at least in California and maybe everywhere is the term prison gangs use to describe their yard chief. "But I was second to the shot caller." He asked, unbidden, for the bartender to give me a shot of tequila. "Get it?" he asked. It took me a minute. Shot caller.

He had short dark hair and I once watched him sit between me and a pretty brunette, who was talking with transparently vulnerable anger to the bartender about how she was out drinking because her some-sort-of-opiate-addict boyfriend had relapsed and she didn't want to go home. Bill said that must be horrible, that he'd had a friend who OD'd in prison but survived, and he said he knew what it was like to care about an addict. He said that after his buddy OD'd they'd found God together, and he asked if she'd like to pray with him. She said she wouldn't mind it, and he took her hand delicately and held it like they were about to waltz at a ball in a Maupassant story. He said the boyfriend would turn out all right, he could feel it. She got up and went to the bathroom, and he ordered two double Jack and Cokes. He turned to me. "I'm gonna fuck her tonight," he said. He did.

The other brother, Eric, seemed to have gotten the family's whole helping of moral focus. He had a trim blond beard and short-cropped hair under a camo ball cap he always wore. I'm not even sure he noticed the women his brother attracted. He talked about three things: his brother, wilderness survival, and politics. I found all of these things interesting, and he seemed to have trouble finding anyone else to talk to, so we sat at the end of the bar while he lectured me, mostly, about how little I knew about rural life, conservation policies, real life in the West, and how to survive when shit really hits the fan. This lecture is more or less the price of entry in rural western bars, and I've learned to just let it happen, but I still find it somewhat in poor taste. I've never lectured a tourist in New York about how little they know about handling themselves in the big city, because on the one hand, who cares, and on the other hand, I figure they hardly need me to point it out. But when you're sitting down and drinking it becomes a sort of masculine power positioning, only a touch more subtle this time around. When I was younger and fresher-faced, it was a bit of a thing for old rancher guys to get a couple of whiskeys in them and ask, "Young man, it's none of my business, but I'm still wondering: do you like boys or girls?" The question isn't in earnest, or it's in earnest on a deeper and angrier level than they want to articulate. It's a pretend lack of sophistication, a way of conveying that they know your tattoos and pants that aren't baggy display a sort of social capital, and it's a way of letting you know that this capital has no play from where they sit.

"Do you have a .22 at home?" Eric asked one night. I did not, at least not then.

"A .22 is the best gun for keeping yourself alive, because there's always going to be small game, even when a deer isn't available, and because the ammo is cheap and easy to store and it used to be widely available before Obama fucked that. So now you're already playing catch-up." This was right at the beginning of the Great Rimfire Ammo Drought, when a box of .22-caliber rounds tripled in price in just a couple of years and Walmart began rationing how many you could buy at a time. It had nothing to do with Obama, but whatever.

"Next, in California, is acorns, because there's always an oak in California. Do you know you have to soak an acorn to get the tannins out?" I said I did. "For how long?" he asked.

"A day?" I said.

"Longer is better," he said. "A day isn't always long enough. And how do you safely store spare gasoline if there's a fuel shortage?" I said I didn't know it was possible to safely store spare gasoline. "It's not," he said. "You get a diesel truck. Is your truck diesel?" I said it wasn't. "Most guys around places like this are gonna have diesel trucks. Is it 4x4?" I said it wasn't but it had a locking rear differential. "That's like saying you don't have a mountain bike but you do have a unicycle," he said. "You need a new truck."

We had both come, along with four thousand other temporary residents, to this little corner of the Sierra Nevada for the occasion of the Rim Fire, which was then burning through the Stanislaus National Forest into Yosemite and would grow into the third-largest wildfire in California's history. I was there with a confused plan to write about the hundreds of California state prisoners working the fire lines, and Eric and his brother did something or other involving servicing parts for vehicles and machinery at the Incident Command Post up the road in Tuolumne City.

This meant we were both working with the Forest Service, which had been extremely accommodating to me even though I didn't have any journalistic assignment or enough money to stay in a motel, and so I had been sleeping in the woods, bathing very occasionally in the Stanislaus River, and drinking every night at the Iron Horse, in the absence of anything better to do.

One night I was getting ready to head up the hill to the forest to sleep, and I said something in passing to Eric about how I hoped I didn't get busted.

"Busted for what?" he asked.

"For camping without a permit," I said.

"What permit?" he asked. I didn't know how to answer this. "It's a national forest, not a fucking playground." He said,

"You can camp wherever the fuck you want." This didn't seem plausible to my eastern brain, and I said so. "Technically, even the idea of a national forest is bullshit," he said, "because it's illegal for the federal government to own land. Did you know that?" I said that now he was sounding like a crank. "Ask anyone," he said. "It's in the Constitution." He turned to an old guy sitting around the bend of the bar from us. "Isn't that true?" he asked him.

"I've heard that," the old man said. "I'm not well-read enough on it myself to say, but I've heard it."

"You a logger?" Eric asked the old man.

"Was," he said.

"Me too," he said. "Was. But now you can't log shit around here, and after this fire is done all the burned timber is going to sit there and rot, because the Forest Service won't even let somebody come in and take the burned trees that are still worth logging."

"That *is* true, and it's bullshit," a loud woman, just after finishing a shot of Fireball, interjected. "The Forest Service is bullshit. They want to ruin this town like they ruin every town."

This was as much as I learned about public lands policy on that trip, but the conversation ended up changing my course in life somewhat drastically. Until then I'd never grasped the difference between a national forest and, say, the state or county parks we had back home in Ohio, where you paid a day rate to enter and counted yourself lucky if you ever got farther than shouting distance from the rest of the campers and hikers who'd come down from Indianapolis or Louisville to drink beer and catch catfish with their buddies. I found it unfathomable, and still do, to realize that if you wanted to you could load up a burro at the edge of Pasadena, pack up into the Angeles National Forest, and march on all the way to Wyoming without ever coming across a No Trespassing sign to stop you, if you planned your route right. I felt like I'd been given a personal gift—I was broke, living in LA, where I knew hardly anyone, had no idea what I was going to do with my life besides drink in redneck bars, and then magically it turned out that I owned half of all the land in the West—45 percent of California, 53 percent of Oregon, 60 percent of Idaho, and on all the way up to 87 percent of Nevada. I especially loved the untrafficked expanse of BLM land, because even as I spent those years without any real home, it felt like I'd been given a way to re-create the special combination of safety and freedom that I'd had in my woods back on the fringes of Cincinnati. I hadn't realized how badly I'd missed it until I found it again. And I didn't mind the ranchers and miners and loggers I met, or think of them as much of an imposition—though if I had been fishing those streams as much as I do now I might have thought differently. I think that most people in my generation have been brought up to think that we don't and can't have public goods in this country, and at first I found it deliriously exciting to see ranchers running cattle on federal ground, a crashing together of collectivism and the most iconic image of free Americana—because who on earth is a more ardent socialist than an American cowboy, pushing horns across 640 million acres of shared public land? It made me very happy to think—to have proof—that these things could coexist.

I put a lot of money on a credit card I had no near hope of paying off, buying topo maps and gas and fishing licenses, and I spent the next two years driving like a madman around the West, halfway lonely out of my mind, and halfway so gleeful I forgot about it, camping in the Sierra away from the crowds of Yosemite and Sequoia, getting my truck stuck in sand down by the border and having to wait three hours for a passing dirt biker to go find help, hanging out in mining camps during the years when the price of gold shot up and broke old guys of all races and from all over America came out west to live in tents and pan for gold. "It's like mountain welfare," a crusty old guy said to me once, as we sat sharing a cigarette by a stream and scanning the ridge above, hoping to see a bighorn sheep. "You just gotta dig for it."

CHAPTER 7

A Brief Historical Aside

In 1907, a wily Basque shepherd named Pierre Grimaud drove his flock over a pass from the edge of the Great Basin onto the western slope of what was then called the Sierra Forest Reserve, only just around the corner from where Eric and I had been drinking. This was illegal, as he knew. The reserve had been established in 1893, the second of dozens of forest reserves cut from free public use under a law signed by Benjamin Harrison in 1891, with the idea mostly of protecting western watersheds from the ravages of clear-cutting, which sent whole hillsides crashing down into streams, fouling rivers, enabling floods, and threatening the growth of Denver, San Francisco, and Los Angeles—all of which depended on the runoff from mountain snowpack for their water supplies. This was the first time that the federal government had taken sections of the big amorphous mass of unclaimed public lands won from Indians or Mexico and had "reserved" them—blocking them from homesteading and unofficially claiming public ownership rather than just stewardship over them until homesteaders or miners or railroads or some other interested party took them private. The implication was that the federal government had the right to manage the lands not solely for individuals who might want to make an economic claim to them, but for the collective good even of people hundreds of miles away.

This didn't go over well. The *Rocky Mountain News* soon described the West as in a "condition of revolt." Loggers and homesteaders ignored the boundaries of the reserves. Western congressmen encouraged their anger, and the big mining and ranching interests sat back, knowing that the politicians would speak for them. The basic lines of the conflict were drawn, even before there were any federal agencies for the "insurgents"—which is a word that had already been applied to anticonservation militants for 130 years before the Bundys ever showed up in the news—to actually fight. Politicians—and even more so the rich benefactors who supported the politicians—found it useful to appear reasonable, but their tools in the press fed the rage of the miners and loggers who thought the reserves were the first step toward tyranny.

Nothing has changed today. "Colorado was overrun with spoilsmen," G. Michael McCarthy, the author of a great, forgotten history of the time, put it. "Like other pioneers, they exalted the idea of the garden, but in their case only as a rationale to justify the monopolization of the land. And, like others, they denounced conservation as immoral, illegal, and destructive of their freedom. . . . It was one of the primary tragedies of the anti-conservation movement that spoilsmen spoke the same language as other westerners."

Then, in 1905, came the Forest Service, under Gifford Pinchot. Pinchot was a taut Pennsylvania aristocrat, who was friends with Teddy Roosevelt and shared the basic bully

Rooseveltian belief in forward human progress, wise and bene-
volent management, and that the cause of freedom was sometimes best served by checking the freedom of the rich to do
whatever it was they wanted to expand their fortunes. Pinchot wanted to manage the forests in the same spirit in which
the reserves had been established—"for the greatest good for
the greatest number," and not necessarily in the immediate
interests of the people using them. The insurgents hated him,
and they already began to talk about armed rebellion.

"The Forest Service is a child of Congress," a Colorado
newspaper editorialized. "Grown up without parental discipline or instruction, an arrogant, bigoted, tyrannical offspring,
the same as any offspring reared in the same manner, void of
respect of law or customs of our land, or the rights and feelings of other people. We now demand the Congress to accept
the responsibility of this outrageous offspring and put the
restraining hand of parenthood to guiding it in the straight and
narrow way before it runs afoul of some sterner justice."

Roosevelt never fully got why he and Pinchot couldn't win
this argument. In 1907, he sent Pinchot to a national Public
Lands Convention in Denver, where he sat for two days while
ranchers and the most powerful politicians in the West lectured
him and insulted his program in a packed, brutally hot, seething hall. "We cannot remain barbarians to save timber," Colorado senator Henry Teller told the crowd. "I do not contend
that the government has the right to seize land, but I do contend that we have the right to put it to the use that Almighty
God intended." When Pinchot finally got up to speak, on the
third day, the crowd booed and jeered as he walked across the

stage. He literally laughed them off. "If you fellows can stand me," he opened with a chuckle, "then I can stand you."

The crowd appreciated this and gave him a cheer at the end, even if he persuaded basically no one. And it's sad to think now how inconceivable it would be for, say, a Democratic interior secretary to go speak to a rowdy crowd of a thousand angry westerners today. The fear wouldn't be that she'd be jeered— it's that she might be assassinated.

Roosevelt and Pinchot convinced most Americans, but they didn't convince most people in the West, where newspapers and politicians and big ranchers resisted conservation less by arguing that it was bad policy, and more by declaring that it was unpatriotic, a betrayal of the American way of life.

"If your ancestors had come to America with mine over 300 years ago," one settler put it in a letter, "if as many of them had fought battles for freedom from King George; if you had been trained in patriotism at the Philadelphia public high school; if you had breathed the spirit of liberty for thirty years on Colorado mountain tops, you would understand and hate 'Pinchotism' as I do. It is diametrically opposed to all true Americanism."

This goes pretty well straight to the point of the issue, which to my mind isn't as much about land use as it is about the great American political poison—the conflation of patriotism with a man's right to make however much money he wants, however he feels like doing it. It's how planters defended slavery, in the name of freedom. It's how they got poor whites to run to their deaths shouting, "Down with the Tyrant," in defense of the most tyrannical institution this country has ever produced. It's how our patricians today defend the oligarchy we all live under. This isn't to say that it's all driven by white supremacism, though it certainly is for some people—especially in the Patriot militias, in ways that they can't or won't fully admit to themselves or see. But everyone is accessing a strand of American history in which economic rights become a sort of synecdoche for a fight over what a free life looks like, and who can claim to be a true American. And if you were to put the story of what was about to come to a tune and sing it, it'd come out sounding a hell of a lot like the old Confederate battle anthem:

> *Oh we're a band of brothers,*
> *native of the soil*
> *fighting for our property,*
> *we gained by honest toil*
> *and when our rights were threatened,*
> *a cry rose near and far*
> *to raise on high the Bonnie Blue Flag,*
> *that bears a single star*

Back then, a few rich southern men, and their enablers in Congress, put forth the idea that an attack on their economic rights was an attack on the whole agrarian way of life. These men funded and owned an alternate and blindly patriotic media. Newspaper editorials and songwriters pushed the idea that the South was the truly American section of the country, that the North had lost touch with the simple yeoman ideal set forth by the founders. The two sections stopped being able to talk to each other. At first, only the remotest fringe of southern radicals—the ones most convinced that not only law but God had blessed their way of life—talked about armed resistance to federal tyranny. But things moved quickly, and by the time the cataclysm arrived it had already come to seem inevitable. There's a process to our sundering, even if it doesn't yet look like a plan.

And they've always left it to the poor to do their fighting. In 1907, Grimaud was caught by rangers as he came over the pass. They asked for his grazing permit and he told them he didn't have one. They took him to court. But he made a canny defense, one he knew would get him support from powerful people: he argued that the rangers had never had the right to stop him in the first place, because the federal government didn't have a right to enforce grazing restrictions on the public lands. Someone—resource bosses had taken a careful interest in the case—stepped up to pay his legal fees, and the case went all the way to the Supreme Court. Finally, after four years, the Court sided with the government. He was convicted, forced to pay a fine, and the right of the USFS rangers to police the reserves was established in law. That should have been the end of it, but of course no part of the public domain is ever really safe in this country.

CHAPTER 8

America Is Zion Itself

The attack began quickly. There's a giant store just off I-15 in Farr West, Utah, outside of Ogden. It's known alternately as "The Everything Store," "The Country Boy Store," and "Smith & Edwards—One Big Adventure," and it was founded in 1947 in the backyard of a young man named Bert Smith, who eventually expanded it to the current sixty-acre site, bought out his partner, and began selling everything from guns to linens. The store became a Utah icon, and Smith became a grand figure in a very Utah sort of way. He had been born in Idaho, was drafted in 1944, and came back to try to work a ranch in Ruby Valley, Nevada, before crossing the desolate flats to buy a place and sell army surplus.

The ranching was hard, and he developed a rage toward the BLM and the Forest Service that followed in a direct line from the anger that grew up around the forest reserves. He was a zealous Mormon, who had helped to set up a new congregation when he moved to Nevada, and he had a special way with people in the Mormon and ranching segment of the Great Basin, where everyone I've met who knew him talks about him with an unguarded reverence.

The store made him rich, and he got into politics. He became a friend and disciple of W. Cleon Skousen, a hyper-Mormon reactionary and former FBI man, who in 1961 had been fired as Salt Lake City's police chief for, as the then mayor put it, running the department "like the Gestapo." Skousen went off to tour the country, giving paranoiac speeches about the communistic menace to American civilization, and he was a key figure in the ferment that led to the nomination of Barry Goldwater, a westerner propelled by forces of reaction and conspiracy so wild that even the candidate himself was bewildered and unnerved by them.

Skousen was his era's boldest and loudest exponent of a basic Mormon belief: that the United States is a chosen land, with a divinely inspired Constitution meant to lead the world into a latter-day libertarian paradise. This was not a new idea. The Book of Mormon itself is the story of lost tribes of Israel who came to the American continent, were visited by Jesus just after the Resurrection, and whose great hero prophesied the American Revolution in the years to come.

"And I beheld the Spirit of the Lord," Nephi says, "that it was upon the Gentiles, and they did prosper and obtain the land for their inheritance; and I beheld that they were white, and exceedingly fair and beautiful, like unto my people before they were slain.

"And I, Nephi," he goes on, "beheld that the Gentiles that had gone out of captivity were delivered by the power of God out of the hands of all other nations."

The holy nature of the founding of this nation is still a basic tenet of the Church. "The whole of America is Zion itself," Joseph Smith said in his time, and the vision carried through to our political system. "I have faith that the Constitution will be saved as prophesied by Joseph Smith," Ezra Taft Benson, who went from being Dwight Eisenhower's secretary of agriculture to the president of the Church, the faith's highest office, told a conference of the Church in 1987. He went on: "I reverence the Constitution of the United States as a sacred document. To me its words are akin to the revelations of God, for God has placed His stamp of approval upon it."

This belief fit comfortably with the views of the non-Mormon extreme right, and the Great Basin became a refuge for paranoid Bircher-style reaction that much of the country thought had been beaten back after the defeat of Goldwater, and for talk that the mainstream right had been busily trying to extirpate in the rest of the country. "There is no doubt," Benson said in 1967, "that the so-called civil rights movement as it exists today is used as a Communist program for revolution in America."

Skousen, who believed in a Rothschild-headed globalist conspiracy against American civilization, and who used the word "pickaninnies" to describe black children, was eventually deemed an inconvenient figure by the Church—which had spent the entire twentieth century trying to show itself to be part of the American mainstream. They barred Mormon clergy from promoting his ideas, even as his admirer Benson rose to Church president. But in 1971, Bert Smith—the rancher-turned-retailer with his revulsion for the BLM—helped Skousen to found a group that eventually became known as the National Center for Constitutional Studies.

The NCCS, backed by Smith's money and Skousen's stature on the extreme right, amalgamated the angry land-use fervor and raging reactionary thought that had been shunted off by the Republican establishment after Goldwater's defeat, and added to them a flavor of Mormon end-times philosophy: there's an enduring belief among some Mormons in a prophecy supposedly articulated by Joseph Smith in 1843, that the Mormon people would "go to the Rocky Mountains" as a "great and mighty people," and that there they would wait, ready, for the time when "you will see the Constitution of the United States almost destroyed. It will hang like a thread as fine as a silk fiber." At this point it would be saved by the efforts of a "White Horse," some righteous person or a collection of them, standing in figuratively for the white horse in the Book of Revelation.

The White Horse Prophecy isn't official Church doctrine, and it's not clear that Joseph Smith even said the words. But the general idea of it, that one day the Constitution would come to hang "by a thread," and that from a western redoubt a group of the righteous would arise to defend it, has had a long and rich life, even outside the confines of Mormonism. Glenn Beck became a disciple of Skousen and loved to reference the prophecy, even on his TV show, watched mostly by Gentiles. And you'll hear and read about the Constitution "hanging by a thread" quite a bit in right-wing circles, once you start to listen out for it.

The NCCS printed tens of millions of pocket Constitutions,

annotated by Skousen to highlight a divine influence on the writing of the document and a subtler implication that threats to it would need to be beaten back in days to come. Bert Smith bought these to distribute for free, a million at a time. I have half a dozen of them now, but I have a special place for the one I got handed to me with my purchase by the friendly young proprietor of a bookstore in Crown Heights, Brooklyn, at the height of the 2016 election. I looked at her in bewilderment, handed it back, and asked if she was trolling me. "It's just a Constitution, don't take it if it offends you." This made it sound very much like she was trolling me—but she looked genuinely confused by my reaction, so we got to talking. It turned out she'd ordered them in bulk online, and had no idea who the NCCS was. Its edition is the first thing that comes up when you search the word "Constitution" on Amazon.

Smith and Skousen became hugely influential in the state, across the West, and in Washington. It was a speech by Skousen, in 1984, that radicalized a young law officer named Richard Mack, who eventually went to Arizona, won election as the sheriff of Graham County, and went on to found a radical group called the Constitutional Sheriffs and Peace Officers Association, which now claims to have five thousand adherents—many if not most of them serving county sheriffs and law officers—pledged to resist, by force if necessary, federal authority on issues like gun control and enforcement of BLM regulations. Mack would go on to be one of the most prominent public supporters of Cliven Bundy.

But Skousen was also close with people such as Utah senator Orrin Hatch, who also has been known to allude in public to the White Horse Prophecy, and who after Skousen's death eulogized him on the Senate floor. He called him, creepily, "the Master Teacher," and even wrote and read out a poem for the occasion. Here is a representative stanza:

> Within this caring, pleasant soul,
> God's glory was refined,
> Experiences had made him whole
> For he had peace of mind,
> So many lives he touched each day
> Explaining holy things,
> In writings left along the way
> A treasure fit for kings.

Smith, meanwhile, became a close friend and patron of Utah congressman Jim Hansen, who eventually rose to become the chairman of the House Committee on Natural Resources, and he gave money to almost every Republican of any stature in the state. He founded and funded his own organization, called the National Federal Lands Conference, which had no website but raised millions of dollars dedicated to resisting federal control of public lands. In 2012 he gave his backing to a group called the American Lands Council, which that same year became the organizing force behind drives in legislatures across the West to demand transfer of public lands from federal to state control. I also noticed once, perusing Federal Election Commission records, that in 2008 he donated a bit of money to the national committee of a tiny fringe grouping called the

Constitution Party. It could just be a coincidence, but that year also happened to be the year when Ryan Bundy ran a long-shot bid for the Utah House of Representatives, on the Constitution Party ticket.

Smith—a confidant of congressmen, funder of governors, and a man who carried enough weight, across state lines, that Ted Cruz even broadcast his endorsement in the run-up to the Nevada presidential caucuses—also called Cliven Bundy a "hero." The pocket Constitutions that the Bundys became known for carrying were always NCCS editions. The path from extremism to the Capitol in this country really isn't so long, once you puzzle it all out. Or the extremism in the Capitol is more present than we like to admit.

CHAPTER 9

Miner Threat

In April 2015, I got an e-mail from a friend and editor of mine containing a link to a story from a tiny local paper in southwestern Oregon, about a standoff brewing between the BLM on one side and a pair of independent gold miners backed by a national paramilitary organization called the Oath Keepers on the other, in the woods north of Grants Pass, a rural and famously lawless corner of the state. I'd just moved back to New York, but he knew I'd spent the last couple of years mostly employed in driving around the West and drinking with rowdy types in rural bars, and he said he thought there could be a story for me. But I'd need to hurry up and get out there if I wanted to see any possible showdown. Some sort of order of noncompliance was supposed to come due in a couple of days.

I said sure, and the next day I was in a rental driving down to Grants Pass from Portland. I got in touch with a miner via Facebook, who told me about a protest that was being held at the BLM/USFS interagency headquarters down the road in Medford, so I went straight there. It was a rainy Friday afternoon, and all the BLM and Forest Service facilities in the area had been closed out of concern for "employee safety." There were about a hundred people, only some of them armed, milling around, holding signs saying "End the BLM" and "Miners' Rights" and "End Fed Tyranny" and things like that, all listening to a speech by Joseph Rice, the head of the local Josephine County Oath Keepers and the impresario of the whole conflagration, speaking from the bed of a white pickup truck. "I took an oath to uphold the Constitution against enemies foreign and domestic," he said from his truck-bed podium. "And a domestic enemy is anyone who'll abuse someone's rights within that Constitution." The soggy crowd cheered. I was lost and annoyed at having flown out, on the theory that only the nuttiest of cranks could really think this small-bore regulatory dispute justified all this talk of tyranny. On the other hand, there were a lot of the nutty cranks, and many of them had come from thousands of miles away, and the depth of feeling seemed meaningful in its own right.

After the speech I went over and introduced myself. Joseph Rice was a former army helicopter pilot, thickly muscled, with a graying beard, an ever present Oath Keepers ball cap, and a hint of a limp in his stride, the result of what he said was a helicopter accident in Afghanistan that had crushed his hip. When I shook his hand he was rigorously polite, in the manner of many military men who are at pains to be respectful even when they have no plans to say very much to you. A few days later, when I asked if it was okay to call him Joe, he said, "I prefer Joseph."

A slightly batty, gray-bearded, and very tan little man came up to him. I didn't know it at the time, but this was Neil Wampler, who would later end up going on trial with Ammon over the Malheur takeover, and who, back in the seventies, when he was twenty-nine, had been convicted of murdering his father in a drunken rage. "I'll do anything at all to help," he said. "I just want to get involved."

Joseph asked if he could cook. He said he could try. "And you know," Neil said, "if there was any chance for some of that more, you know, tactical training, I would be ready for that." Joseph said he'd let him know.

I asked Joseph if I'd be able to go up to the encampment the Oath Keepers had set up around the mine. "No," he said. "That won't be possible." Then he got pulled away again and I went to introduce myself to the more voluble of the two gold miners—a giant, wild-looking, and raucous guy with a big beard and crazy teeth named Rick Barclay. He had a claim on a small hard-rock mine called the Sugar Pine, which had been worked on and off by miners in the area for more than a hundred years. He'd paid $10,000 for the claim, and brought up a bulldozer to grade roads, and built a cabin and a stamp mill to process ore, and had gone to work. No one disputed that he had a valid claim on the mine itself, but mining law and public lands regulations covering minerals management are so complicated that even the people in charge of their administration can barely grasp them all—there are literally thousands of laws that touch on mining on public lands, and that's not even beginning to consider the tens of thousands of BLM and Forest Service orders and regulations—and so there was a dispute about whether he had rights to the *surface* of the mine, on which he'd need to run his dozer or build structures at the site. Mines that have had continuous title since before the 1955 Surface Resources Act all have surface rights grand-fathered in. Mines that haven't been in continuous operation have to file a Plan of Operations with the BLM, stating what they plan to do and assessing environmental impacts, which can take time and cost money and which Rick—who had never been much of a lover of written communication—wasn't inclined to do anyway. He didn't file one, BLM had found him to be breaking the rules, and things kind of went from there. Rick had a bunch of government documents and old papers signed by long-dead miners to show that the Sugar Pine had been in continuous operation; the BLM had a bunch of government documents and old papers showing it hadn't. Rick told them to go to hell, and the BLM said it was going to deliver him a notice of noncompliance on April 25, two days from when we were talking.

This is when the guns came out. He had asked the Oath Keepers—who had enjoyed something of a coming-out party at an earlier standoff with the BLM at the Bundy family ranch in Nevada, which we'll get to—to come out because he seemed genuinely worried that the BLM had a history of acting first and justifying later. "What they'll do is come in and burn stuff and haul your stuff out before your court date," he said. "And that's bullshit." I asked if he wasn't just bullshitting me. "There's an endless variety of folks," he said, who'd had this happen to them. He named some. It's not the sort of thing you can ask an agency for records on—"Do you have any files on your employees going around and illegally burning the homes of miners and loggers?" And so he could have been just naming cranks and idiots with a beef, or he could have been speaking a truth, or maybe it could have been somewhere in between. It was true that even the girl behind the desk at the Motel 6, a twentysomething who'd never mined a day in her life, could name miners she said had been burned out of their cabins. "I was here in the eighties when they were burning everything in sight," Rick said. "Both agencies did it—that phenomenon doesn't know any boundaries.

"The only reason my stuff is still standing," he said, "is that there's guys saying we'll shoot you if you fucking burn us down. If you don't want your nose broke, keep it out of my business."

CHAPTER 10

Bureau of Livestock and Mines

The rain picked up and the protest ended. I met up with a photographer, Shawn Records, who became my more or less constant companion through the adventures of the next year, and who through all of it was always the sanest person in the room. He'd never done any journalism before, he'd never met me, and ended up on this trip only because some photo editor found him on Facebook, but within the year he was trundling in his silver Tacoma to the darkest corners of the state and I'd open the *Times* and see his shots right there at the top of the home page. A week before he'd been shooting condos for a real estate catalog. He had two boys back in Portland and had some impossibly disarming soft-spoken cool-dad charm that made everyone like him almost before he said his name, which half the time was all he ever said. He could have asked a hissing cat to hold a pose for a minute while he changed lenses. We went to meet up with a contact at the local BLM, a public information officer named Jim Whittington. He said he was happy to meet in person, and I suggested he swing by the interagency office, since the protest was over and Shawn and I were already sitting in the parking lot.

He paused and said vaguely that meeting there would be "ah . . . inconvenient." He asked if I knew anywhere else in the area. I'd seen a Starbucks down the road and suggested that as an option, and he said he knew the place. "We can meet you there in fifteen minutes," he said, as though he'd been driving around waiting for a dispatch call.

It was still spitting rain and chilly, but the Starbucks wouldn't let Shawn take pictures inside, so we set up under an umbrella at an outside table. Whittington, whom I recognized from photos I'd seen on some rather sinister antigovernment blog posts, approached with a man who surveyed the scene and pronounced it satisfactory. We said we were sorry about the rain and cold, but Whittington waved away the apology. "No, I was going to suggest that we talk out here anyway," he said. "Inside people could hear things that . . ." He trailed off. It felt very much like a drug deal.

The other man introduced himself as Tom Gorey, a higher-level public affairs official who'd been rushed in by Washington to run point on the events at the mine. This seemed reasonable—Whittington had sounded harried and exhausted both times I'd spoken with him on the phone. I had read vilifications of him (representative title of a pro-miner blog post: "IS BLM SPOKESMAN JIM WHITTINGTON A COMPULSIVE LIAR? DOES HE NEED PROFESSIONAL HELP?") and would hear similar assessments of him and Gorey, coloring them as stooges or malign manipulators, depending on who was doing the describing. But they were more or less exactly what you'd expect from public affairs people working on environmental issues for a government agency: Whittington was soft-spoken and wore a dad-who-hikes sort of green fleece vest; Gorey, a tough-looking man who was getting up in his years and had clearly dealt with his share of angry westerners, was gruffer and slightly more officious, but only slightly. They were friendly and reasonable, but they were also the public representatives of a government facing a genuine challenge to its legitimacy, and they were unable to meet us in the offices of that government housed half a mile down the road. The situation was beyond absurd.

The BLM is an unfortunate little agency. It was created by Congress as an imperfect answer of what to do with the unreserved public lands left over after the creation of the national forests, after homesteading slowed down, and after various administrations tried and failed to figure out a way to give them over to the states. Hoover tried this, and it's funny now to read the then governor of Utah's angry protestations, when today every major elected official in the state acts like the government came in and stole the land from them: the western states had "millions of acres of this same kind of land," he said, "which they can neither sell nor lease, and which is yielding no income. Why should they want more of this precious heritage of desert?"

"They say we got the lands nobody wanted," Whittington said, slightly defensively. But part of why nobody wanted them was that the BLM used to be an agency staffed by the sons of ranchers, miners, and loggers, and mostly it was interested in helping the neighbors make a living on the land as easily as they could. No one cared who owned the lands, because they were easy to use. Conservationists used to mock it as the Bureau of Livestock and Mines, and its original logo—you can't make this stuff up—was a pen-and-ink drawing of a miner, a rancher, a logger, and an oilfield engineer marching side by side with a BLM surveyor through a clear desert toward a vista, meant to represent the future, of oil wells and smoking factories.

This began to change in the sixties, when the bureau began hiring professional range and minerals technicians, changed the logo to a vista of a river flowing down from a pristine mountain, and began asking Congress to give it something like the mandate for multiple-use conservation that the Forest Service had. The Forest Service, for all the people who resented it, had a great institutional pride and camaraderie. People were proud to work for it, and they threw fun parties for the wives and families living together up at the ranger stations, and the lands they managed had a name—they were the national forests, people could see them on a map, they visited them, they met friendly rangers, and they knew Smokey the Bear. People visited from all over the country, and they appreciated the rangers and the forests.

But mining interests, ranchers, and western politicians had always managed to block moves to turn the BLM into something similar. The lands have always been hard to visualize—in the 1960s not even the agency director had a working map of the lands he was charged with managing. Even today, sixty years after the bureau was created, it's hard to even talk about or conceive of public lands, because western congressmen have blocked any attempt to name them—they're just "BLM land," and who wants to tell the kids that you're taking them on a trip to BLM land? This was intentional: the point was to keep people from visiting and falling in love with the lands, and to leave them clear for the miners and ranchers and drillers.

Eventually Congress broke this system down, almost by accident. It passed the Endangered Species Act, the National Environmental Policy Act, and a whole list of other laws requiring federal agencies to take new environmental standards into account when they made their decisions. These, to my mind, are all pretty necessary laws, but it seems unlikely that Congress thought through their full implications. All of a sudden the BLM found itself protecting landscapes from people who a few years before it'd treated like honored guests. The bureau had no clear legal mandate to do this, and so in 1976 Congress passed the Federal Land Policy and Management Act, which repealed the Homestead Act, finally clarifying that the federal government was going to take ownership of the public lands, and giving the BLM something like the Forest Service's mandate to be a steward of the land, not just a facilitator of economic use. It also gave the agency policing powers like those the Forest Service had established way back in the early 1900s, to patrol the forest reserves.

This produced a pure and hot kind of rage, the kind that derives from a sense of betrayal. The immediate result was the Sagebrush Rebellion, a revolt led by western legislatures against federal environmental regulations. The lasting result was that as the BLM began restricting grazing and logging and everything else a great number of people who'd always been friends and neighbors with BLM employees started to see the agency as part of an environmentalist plot to take their livelihoods, force people off the land, destroy rural communities, and turn the entire West into a manicured playground for bighorn sheep and hikers from Boston. And it's true that this is a pretty fair picture of what some people want, and that some seem driven more by a cultural distaste for ranchers and rednecks than they are by a desire to challenge the larger forces that threaten the lands of the West. The Forest Service got caught up in the conflict too. Ranger stations were bombed, BLM employees threatened, and eventually, quietly, this became normal. Between 2010 and 2014 there were fifty antigovernment attacks on BLM or Forest Service employees, including two assassination attempts by snipers on Forest Service employees in 2013. It divided a lot of communities—places where almost everyone either works for one of the land agencies or works on the land, or does both. There were and are a lot of good people caught in the middle. And there were and are a lot of irreconcilables who looked at the BLM, looked at the widening divide in the whole country, looked at the gaining purchase of militant and extremist constitutional ideas across the West and wanted to provoke a crisis on a national scale. This is where the Bundy family stepped up.

CHAPTER 11

Whatever It Takes

The immediate Bundy family constitutes Cliven, his second wife, Carol, seven sons, and seven daughters, and now sixty-three grandchildren. Ryan is the oldest and by far the roughest in his bearing—his face twisted into a permanent grimace from a childhood accident when he was hit by a car, which stalled out on his head before the driver gunned the engine, cracking his skull and severing a nerve that controls the motor function on the left side of his face. He was seven years old. He speaks with a slow, deep lilt, which disguises somewhat how brash and uncompromising he is. He once pulled his kids out of public school because his daughter was barred from carrying a pocketknife to class. At the refuge he was always casually tossing off lines like "It's gonna get violent" or "Guns show we're serious," which then Ammon would have to walk back.

Ammon, three years younger, is subtler and more measured, and is unquestionably his generation's leader, though he'd deny it. He's just as uncompromising in his beliefs as Ryan but has a more natural sense of persuasion and a very soft-spoken, humble, outward affect. The two make a powerful combination, and have since they were teenagers growing up on the ranch. Even then they had a reputation as being impossible to persuade, and of being sure they were capable of anything they wanted to do. I asked Ammon once if he'd been a wrestler in high school, and it turned out—or at least this is what Carol told me later—that he'd been an untrained boxer. In high school he and Ryan decided to enter a toughman fight tournament, up the highway in Saint George, Utah. They practiced against each other in the backyard, and when the day came the brothers won all their matches until the semifinals, when Ryan pulled out with a torn ligament, which may have been a pretext so the brothers wouldn't have to face each other in the final. Ammon won the championship. "He came home and set the ten hundred-dollar bills on the table," she told me. "I asked if it had been worth it and he said no—it should have been more money."

Members of the family have been in Clark County since 1877, when they descended the Virgin River gorge from Utah to Nevada, in a secondary wave of Mormon settlement. They're rather tough people now, and they would have been tougher then. The gorge, which you would travel along if you ever drive I-15 from Las Vegas toward Salt Lake City, is cut by the river as it descends from the sagebrush highlands around Saint George and flows into a rough transition zone between the Great Basin and Mojave Deserts. Around the Nevada line the sagebrush mostly ends, the creosote bush takes over, and the river emerges silty and green into a narrow plain of yellow rock. The ranch is just off the highway in Bunkerville, a few exits inside the Nevada line. It, like Las Vegas, is in Clark County. Without traffic it's less than a two-hour drive from the Las Vegas Strip, though of course it feels two worlds away.

I missed the standoff, because at the time I didn't have the gas money to go, but I've been to Bunkerville many times— passing through, to visit the ranch, and once to buy a rifle I found a good deal on at a pawnshop. I spent a long time there, getting my background check and chatting with the two women running the place. One, a Hispanic woman in her thirties who lived up the road in Saint George, mentioned the Bundys, and I mentioned that I knew them, and she shook her head in bafflement. "Everything else aside, I mean—this?" she said, and waved her hand out to indicate the landscape. "God's chosen land?" I love some of the plants on the ranch, and one of my favorite times I've spent in the family orbit was an afternoon driving around with one of Cliven's sons-in-law, checking out grasses and identifying wildflowers after an unusually wet spring. But it's mostly just creosote bush and bare yellow rock, broken only by a thick clutch of invasive and horribly destructive tamarisk trees down along the Virgin River, which runs thin and sluggish—a mix of cloudy gray from silt and pale green from farm runoff—down the wide valley toward Lake Mead, and even on a hot day doesn't seem very inviting.

The family bought 160 deeded acres and developed their own breed of cattle, good for the desert—tough little hump-backed Brahman cows with gorgeous coloration that looks uncannily like polished tiger's-eye stone. And after the Grazing Service came into existence, in 1934, they claimed grazing rights on a vast section of the Gold Butte allotment.

They continued on mostly unmolested until the late '80s,

when ranchers in Clark County began to go out of business more or less en masse. This was at the beginning of a new and flintier conflict over land use in the West, when ranchers began to feel like they were living through an environmentalist intifada, and environmental groups began to sense that with tools such as the Endangered Species Act—and sometimes by more forceful means—they had it within their power to end logging and ranching on public lands entirely. The group Earth First!, which had been founded in the 1980s as a crusty western direct action group inspired by Edward Abbey's novel *The Monkey Wrench Gang*, was growing into an anarchist-inflected movement that eventually led to the creation of the more intensely militant Earth Liberation Front. It terrified ranchers, who probably credited the group with being much more powerful than it actually was.

"Ranchers blame environmental extremists for scattered acts of vandalism and violence on ranches in the West," the *Times* reported in 1991, interviewing a rancher across the line in Utah. "A year ago, 24 cows and calves were shot to death on Mr. Lyman's ranch. Not long before the killings, Mr. Lyman found a sign placed on his ranch that read: 'Stop Destructive Welfare Ranching.'"

The fight was already on, if anyone cared to notice. "I told them, now you can't go shoot somebody just because you want to," the local sheriff was quoted as saying in the same piece. "And I think most of the ranchers understood that."

Some ranchers began to see the government and the environmental movement as two arms of a pincer movement out to destroy them. "I'm concerned about the safety of my employees," a Nevada Forest Service district manager told the *Washington Post* around that time. "They can't go to church in these communities without having someone say something. Their kids are harassed in school. Stores and restaurants are not serving them."

In the 1980s there were fifty-two ranchers running cattle in Clark County. But in 1989 the desert tortoise, during a noisy push for listings by environmental groups that had adopted the spirit and goals, if not the exact tactics, of Earth First!, was listed under the Endangered Species Act. This created a problem for Las Vegas and surrounding municipalities, because in order for them to expand, they had to encroach on the habitat of a now protected species, and for the BLM, which managed most of the surrounding desert, that now had to protect tortoise habitat against both present and potential threats.

The most obvious threat to the tortoise was urban development, but the county government didn't really have any interest in trying to contain that. So the county sought out and got an agreement with the US Fish and Wildlife Service that allowed a waiver for development in the Las Vegas Valley in exchange for commitments to preserve tortoise habitat elsewhere in the county. And what this amounted to was getting ranchers off that land. "Clark County made a choice," James Skillen, author of *The Nation's Largest Landlord*, a surprisingly engaging and balanced history of the BLM, told Reuters in 2014. "Urban development is far more important to us than ranchers on the periphery of the county."

I tend to think that extremism in defense of an endangered species is no vice, but what happened in Clark County is a good example of why this debate can be so brutally contentious. Soon after the tortoise was listed, the BLM issued an emergency rule cutting spring grazing on the Clark County range. A group of ranchers sued, arguing that no one had established that cattle and tortoises couldn't coexist, and a court found in favor of the ranchers. The BLM quickly offered a second, reworded grazing order.

The ranchers sued and won again. In 1994 the Fish and Wildlife Service issued a report saying that the "extremely controversial" question of whether or not cattle on the range were a threat to tortoise habitat was still up in the air. In 2002 the US Geological Survey issued its own report saying that the case that cattle had much impact on tortoise habitat was "not overwhelming." Whereas the case that the expansion of a metropolis that would grow in population from 770,000 in 1990 to almost 1.5 million in 2000—with all the ranch houses and in-ground pools that came with it—hurt the tortoises' habitat was so obvious that it barely needed any examination. An environmentalist could probably say, fairly, that these reports would need to be taken with some skepticism, because these agencies had a history of treating the sensibilities of ranchers very gently. A rancher could say, fairly, that he was made the object of a political project to drive ranchers off the range in Clark County—which is true, plain and simple. This isn't to say they had any more right to the range than the tortoise or a hiker visiting Vegas from Marin, who wants to hike up on Gold Butte and look at wildflowers without having to see cow patties and stock tanks while he does it. But it's not as though you couldn't go hike or camp on land where the

Bundys were running their cattle, as they're very quick to point out and repeat constantly. Ranchers don't have a right to seal off public land where they graze their stock, and the whole happy principle of multiple use on public lands is that it's supposed to be a sort of managed coexistence between the interests of nature, such that it has any, and the various competing interests of people who want to use the land, whether it be for viewing wildflowers or mining for uranium. In practice it's usually money and access to politicians that decides who wins these arguments. And in Clark County the interests of the ranchers lost out. Mostly.

The BLM and US Fish and Wildlife took the line that it was time to ease the ranchers out. Even without the clearance orders, they began slashing AUMs on the grazing allotments and offering buyouts. Some ranchers took buyouts willingly, because they were getting on in years and their kids didn't want to take over and it was a hard life and why not take a bit of cash and move on? But some took them because they felt like they didn't have another option. Some couldn't afford to keep going after the AUMs were cut and they were allowed to run fewer cattle on public ground, in country where it takes at least a hundred acres of ground to run a cow and calf pair. The math on that is that it takes thirty thousand acres to run an extremely modest ranch of three hundred head of cattle. In Clark County the idea of ranchers surviving in business without running on public ground is just a joke—it would be impossible to buy the acreage. So it's true that the government was able to control, for better or worse, the shape of their futures. And some just got worn down. "I couldn't afford to pay the lawyers when they keep taking you to court," Calvin Adams, who used to ranch with the Bundys on the Bunkerville allotment, told Reuters in 2014. He took a $75,000 buyout and quit ranching. Meanwhile, a report issued in 2001 by the county gave an estimate that four hundred tortoises had been killed *every year* by building projects after the tortoise management plan had been enacted.

In 1993 Cliven Bundy wrote a short letter to the BLM, notifying the agency that he wanted to cancel all his contracts, and that from then on he would be happy to pay grazing fees to Clark County, but that he would do no more business with the federal government. The BLM didn't know what to do, and it barely did anything, besides fine him. He didn't pay the fines. Every other rancher in the county folded up, but Cliven raised and sold his cattle, branched out into melon farming, and went along in his way. And there isn't much evidence that the BLM or anyone really cared. He was fined. He declined to pay the fines. He was fined again. Nothing happened.

In the meantime, Cliven had worked up a philosophy, which was partly cribbed from Mormon theology, partly from Skousenite and extreme right-wing thought, and partly a product of his own belief in revelation and his family's experience with the government. The family developed—and now that every one of the older males has sat for two years in pretrial detention—a bit of a persecution complex. But their religion, and the messianic tendencies of Cliven, which Ammon soon adopted, gave the persecution complex a sort of universalist flair—you can hear it in the way they talk that much of what was to come was driven by the reactive anger of a true, deep egotist facing adversity. Most people experience adversity as personal misfortune, or even maybe as a product of their own past missteps. The Bundy men experience personal misfortune as evidence that something is wrong with the world around them. And rather than change themselves, they set out to change what was wrong with that world.

Cliven and Ryan—who stayed close to the ranch while Ammon moved off to start a trucking maintenance business in Arizona—spent the decades after they voided their BLM contracts building networks and sensing the anger of people like Shawna Cox, who had come into the radical side of land politics after the creation of the Grand Staircase–Escalante National Monument up near the Utah-Arizona line, and would later become one of the hardest-to-place characters in the Bundy movement. She's an unbelievably energetic sixty-year-old woman with a cascade of unruly platinum hair, thirteen children, and nearly four dozen grandchildren, one of whom had just tragically and suddenly died the day before we were speaking, and has been married three times—once to the brother of the man she was married to before, after the first husband died in a car accident.

She lives in Fredonia, Arizona—just across the line from Kanab, Utah, and just up the road from LaVoy Finicum's family ranch—and with the man she's been married to since 1990 runs a sprawl of businesses around town: a mobile home rental company, a motel, a car dealership—I'm not even sure what all else, but there are more. She's very religious and very up front about it, prone to wild conspiracy theories, and a deep believer that the Bundy cause is less a fight over land use than it is something closer to a battle for the soul of a civilization. She'd known Cliven and Ryan Bundy casually for years, but like so many people who came into contact with the family at the family ranch in 2014, she fell into the role of a fervid loyalist, living at the ranch for months after the standoff, and eventually falling into a spiritually manic phase during which she wrote a hagiographical book about Cliven called *Last Rancher Standing.*

For the so-called Patriot movement, she's become half chronicler of events and half someone who has been at the heart of the action without ever herself claiming to have played much of a role in anything. Over time we've gotten to know each other, and because we've followed the same things for so long, if from totally different mind-sets, I find that it can be fun, if slightly madcap, to pass the time with her.

I happened to cross paths with her a year or so after the standoff, met her in Texas Station casino in North Las Vegas, which seemed like a funny place for a proselytic Mormon woman to suggest that we meet up. But it was close to the safe house where she was staying, which was well kept and basically similar to the rest of the houses in the one-story sea of North Vegas, with the slight alteration that it was built underground with a hatch in the gravel instead of a door, it had well-hidden skylights instead of windows, and you accessed it behind the locked fence of a building-supply yard. She and some others were using it as a base of operations during the trials, which were being held in downtown Las Vegas. I took my coffee with her there the next morning and asked who owned the place. She shook her head like I ought to have known better. "Someone in the movement" is all she said.

She told me about getting an e-mail from Cliven in April 2012 and being taken aback, because she had hardly heard from him since they met back in the 1990s. "'They're coming to pick up my cows and shut us down,'" she said he wrote to her. "'And we'll do whatever it takes. I got my family here. We'll do whatever it takes to stop them.'" She started calling everyone she knew, telling them to get ready. She said she'd never met any of the Bundys besides Cliven and Ryan, and them only briefly. She had never been to the ranch. But she was ready to roll and assembled people to come with her. The government seemed to have been caught off guard by the storm Cliven was able to call. The next morning at 6:00 a.m., he phoned Shawna and told her that the operation had been called off. "But it's postponed," she said. "It's not really over."

And when, two years almost to the day after the false alarm in 2012, the BLM called to say people were coming in for real this time, they were ready. There are recordings of the phone call. A BLM agent called the house and spoke to Ryan, asking if "there was going to be any kind of, you know, *physical* issue."

"The best way to avoid that is to not come in here," Ryan told him. "I will do whatever it takes, and I will have several hundred supporters with me to help." They love this phrase. This time, when Cliven put out the call, people came en masse. News spread first through the underground networks of the rural West—a phone call to a rancher, who called his nephew, who called his sister-in-law. The younger ones spread it on Facebook. Shawna was there in a day. LaVoy Finicum came. Stanton Gleave, the portly kingpin of Piute County, Utah, came with his horse and his stature as a Mormon patriarch, and friends and followers came in their wake. The cowboys the BLM hired to execute the roundup were threatened with death and worse. "We were hot and ready, man, 'cause we knew some of those people," one guy told me. "Where we live, I mean, you know what they do to cattle rustlers in the West, right? We took that as cattle rustling."

An Internet radio personality named Pete Santilli, who later ended up being the very first face I saw at the Oregon standoff, showed up and started broadcasting the call on his livestreamed show. Things got wild. Glenn Beck started talking about it. The Patriot militias started showing up. This was the emergence of the movement. Militias and hard-line armed right-wing groups had been growing like scattered dandelions in this country since the election of Barack Obama, from around a hundred in 2008 to over a thousand in 2013. But they lived, to put it simply, in the political shadow of the militia movement of the 1990s—always at pains to make the case that they weren't white supremacists, and the whole thing marked by the enormity of the Oklahoma City bombing. They desperately wanted a cause to latch onto, and Cliven gave it to them. "We didn't ask for the militias to come," Carol Bundy told me, one day at the ranch. "But we were happy they did! I mean, we were just alone out here, with women and children. And we didn't know what they were going to do."

The Oath Keepers, led by their founder, Stewart Rhodes,

came. The Idaho III% came. Ryan Payne, who would be the quiet hard-line force behind what happened in Oregon, came with his Montana militia. Hundreds of people came, and some unknowable but large portion of them brought guns. At least three sheriffs—serving county sheriffs in charge of enforcing the law for tens of thousands of people each—came, from Indiana, Kentucky, and Delaware.

The BLM, which had a strong institutional desire to handle the roundup itself, brought a tactical team headed by a special agent named Dan Love—who even before this had taken on a reputation as the most hated man in the angrier precincts of the rural West. He's tall and wears a dark crew cut and a thick, short beard and Oakley sunglasses. He has since been fired, after allegedly giving away artifacts that were evidence in a looting case, and using his position to demand free tickets and luxury accommodations at Burning Man. His plan was to round up the cattle quickly, and to do it in such force that even if things got tense it would be too late for protesters to stop them. But he hadn't anticipated this being the outlet for a new culture of American insurgency. Within a few days hundreds of people were there. Cliven's scattered sons had rushed home—Ammon from Arizona, Mel and Dave, a quieter and less political pair, from Utah and a remote mining job. Cliven had a force at his command larger than many guerrilla armies. His messianic tendencies had an outlet. The Clark County sheriff tried to defuse the situation. This didn't work. Later Cliven would stand the sheriff up on stage, with cameras from every TV network in the country rolling, and lecture him about a revelation he'd received, that the sheriff would roll up and seize the guns of Park Service rangers at the gates of Lake Mead. "You take a pickup, and I want those arms—we want those arms—picked up, don't we?" he said, to howls of approbation from the crowd. The sheriff, mortified, surrounded, and noticeably less of a physical presence than Cliven, who was fifteen years older than he was, said nothing about how this was both crazy and impossible and tried and failed to look professional.

And Ammon came fully into his own. This isn't speculation—you can see him in the video footage, clean-shaven and thinner than he would appear up in Oregon, wearing a straw cowboy hat and bouncing around in pickup trucks talking to reporters. "What will you do if they come back?" one, clearly fawning Fox News stringer asked him. "We do this right," he said, "and they won't come back."

It took several days to assemble the protesters—or the private army, depending on how you want to look at it. At this point the events at the ranch had become front-page news across the country. Senators including Ted Cruz and Dean Heller went on TV and radio to support the family, though they backed off after Cliven made comments to the effect that black Americans might have been better off living under slavery than in public housing. Harry Reid—a Mormon from another tiny Clark County desert town—denounced them passionately and clearly took the whole thing as an almost personal affront, but the situation by now was out of hand as hundreds were encamped in the rocky hills around the ranch, and more people were flowing in every day. Cliven didn't get the guns from Lake Mead—not that he forgot about it. "The message I gave to you all was a revelation I received," he lectured from the stage later. "And yet not one of you can seem to even quote it."

But he got a more proximate victory. As the numbers swelled and the Bundys grew more confident, they decided that the hundreds of cattle the BLM had managed to impound needed to be freed. And so they came up with a plan. The cows and calves—in the instances where the BLM had managed to actually keep cows with their calves—were being held in a corral a few miles up the river and interstate from the ranch. Cliven got up on the stage with his microphone again. "And all we gotta do," he announced, "is open the gate and turn 'em back on the river and they're home. But we're going to need a bit of safety here."

He directed the little army to seize the interstate, which cut over the wash as an overpass right where the cattle were being kept. "We're gonna block the freeway," he said. "When we get to the bridge we're gonna get out of our cars." The plan was to put the militia force in a spot, no matter that it happened to be a major American artery of traffic and commerce, where it could have undisputed high ground facing off against BLM agents stuck defending a corral, which clearly hadn't been set up with siege defense in mind. Riders on horseback were going to ride down the river and come up the wash, covered by snipers from the bridge, and confront the BLM head-on. Cliven waved his hand casually. "Go get 'em cowboys." Everyone set off.

They took the highway and the cowboys rode out. Dan

Love moved his tactical team, wearing helmets and carrying long guns and generally looking like they were geared more for action in Kandahar than in Nevada, into defensive positions in the wash. People on foot started catching up with the cowboys who'd arrived on horseback and collecting in the wash among them. The word spread through the crowd that if anyone advanced toward the BLM they'd be shot, and that possibly the BLM was planning to start shooting anyway. Shawna and I talked about it at the casino.

"Ammon was there, and he stopped me, and he goes, 'Don't go over there, they've got guns up there,'" she said. "And because I'm a curious animal, I had to go over there and take a picture, and sure enough, they were there with their guns pointing down the wash."

If it's really true the BLM agents were aiming guns, the Bundyites certainly reciprocated. E. J. Parker, a member of the Idaho III% whom I met at the Sugar Pine, and whom I'd later see at the Malheur standoff, became the face of this moment, when he lay down on the asphalt of the I-15 bridge and sighted his AR through a break in the concrete sidewalls. A Reuters photographer captured an amazing side view of him aiming out toward the BLM position, a photo that would lead to him being charged with felonies that could have put him in prison for the rest of his life. Jury deliberations in his trial were going on while Shawna and I were talking at the casino. But the real action was below. Ammon led, per usual. "And so Ammon says, 'Let's wait till everyone gets down the road and we'll have a prayer.'" They assembled, and Shawna spoke it. "Please help us," she said, "as we go about this task. That we will be safe, and we invoke thy power to defend us. We ask these things humbly, and in the name of thy Son Jesus Christ."

There was a rousing cheer of *Amen*, and then Ammon's voice rose up. "We'll get some courage," he said. "And then we'll ask them to . . . er, *demand*, that they leave."

"It didn't have a thing to do with me," Shawna told me later. "I just was moved to say the things I said. Anyway, and I knew that was our protection. We all felt that, we all felt that protection."

Then the same fawning Fox News stringer, playing hero, approached the corral, waving a white flag. BLM agents using a megaphone ordered him back. He kept coming forward. Dan Love, wearing a backward baseball cap and his Oakleys, came to the fence of the corral. He asked for Ammon, who approached. The camera was rolling in their faces, and Love was clearly keyed up on adrenaline, worried there was going to be gunfire, talking fast and pausing at times to take a breath. Ammon was absurdly calm. Love offered to withdraw, but he said he needed Ammon to back the crowd up so he could get his team out safely. "No," Ammon said. "This is state of Nevada land. You leave now." They did. All the cattle were released. The family went on ranching.

This was the beginning of a new kind of extralegal politics, one that would extend far beyond the contours of western land conflicts. For the Oath Keepers and the new militia movement it provided a proof of concept—they could get things done and outmuscle the federal government. The organization now claimed to have thirty thousand members and took on the Bundy cause as its own, without hiding at all that it saw the movement as a step toward opening a wider conflict in American society. Now, after the election of Trump, its members are at it almost every week, working as a sort of paramilitary pro-Trump strike force. They've dedicated themselves to infiltrating left-wing protest groups and standing with neo-Nazis and Alt-Right groups like the Proud Boys in street fights against Antifa, with an obvious but not fully stated aim to goad the anti-Trump left into a spiral of violence heading toward some sort of apocalyptic reckoning.

They're very careful about policing their words now. But Stewart Rhodes has made it very clear that this has been the goal all along, and that it started at the Bundy ranch.

"The whole Bundy family, and many of their cowboy friends and neighbors were willing to take a hard stand," Rhodes wrote later. "With the support of veterans and patriots, they prevailed, the Feds blinked, and backed off. That was a clear win for Team Liberty, while maintaining the moral high ground in the eyes of the great majority of patriotic Americans—which is exactly why the Feds backed off. They knew they had overstepped, that the 'optics' were bad, and they had severely underestimated the resolve and resistance, and could not win without using overwhelming military force. And they knew that if they tried to use that military force—as many leftists were screaming for them to do—the military would split at least in half, and many or most of the current serving trigger pullers in the Marine Corps and Army infantry would have sided with the resistance—joining all of us pissed off veterans in the resulting civil war."

CHAPTER 12

Coyote Down

This is what the BLM was facing in Oregon. "All that happened was that we made a finding of noncompliance," Tom Gorey told me that afternoon, under a spring drizzle. "Since the situation we're in is they're saying, 'Oh, no, we do have surface,' then they can file an appeal. There was never an issue of due process," he said. "Nothing is going to happen to their structures.

"Their line that they've been peddling is that the BLM was going to go in there and set fire to the cabin, take the equipment, and all this was going to happen before they went to court," he said.

I asked Whittington about the burning of structures. "That has happened in the past," he said. "If you look back in the 1970s, you had all these guys who were basically putting up a cabin and saying it was attached to a mine. They were basically homesteading." This didn't necessarily go against the prevailing theory that land managers want people out of the woods. "There were a lot of old rickety cabins out there, and we did burn cabins. We've maybe burned one in the last fifteen years.

"Their narrative is that the BLM's a bully and federal thugs and strongmen are coming in to trample on their rights. But it's just a false narrative." He knew that the resentment had come from somewhere, and he had been in the agency long enough to see how far it went: "The desire of many is, 'Hey, you're locking up the lands, and we can't use them the way we did,' " he said. "Wilderness designations and the success of the environmental movement have put restrictions, and there's been this resentment. You combine it with far-fetched constitutional interpretations, things like that county sheriffs are the major players in government—I mean that's what you're running up against." I asked whether the BLM might move in with force. "We're the government," he said. "We're good at sending letters."

I asked him what the future looked like for an agency that risked starting a revolution every time it tried to tell a camper to recycle his beer bottles. "Good luck to the militia movement to disestablish the federal government," he said. "We may have lost the battle of Bundyville, but we will win the war."

Shawn and I spent most of the next few days with a woman named Mary Emerick. She was a retired high school principal from Diamond Bar, California, with a manicured sandy-blond hairdo and a grandmother's resigned concern for everyone around her. She seemed like an unlikely antigovernment warrior, and it was hard at first to see how she'd gotten involved in all this. But she was also Joseph's right hand, and when we made it clear that he wouldn't be able to get rid of us, he'd told us to talk to her.

The next morning she called and invited us to see a press

conference, held by a crowd of concerned citizens on the steps
of the Josephine County courthouse, on the downtown strip
of Grants Pass. There were about twelve people up on the
steps, waiting for the local TV cameras to get set up. Joseph
and Mary stood off to the back with a man named Brandon
Curtiss, the head of the Boise-based Idaho III%.

The speakers began to talk one by one, and they mostly
addressed Joseph directly. A former dean of the local community college asked him to "let the legal process, rational dis-
course, and old-fashioned negotiation determine a nonviolent
outcome—for the good of all of us." A sporting-goods dealer
named Dave Strahan got up and called the militiamen a bunch
of "nutty, tough-acting, gun-toting thugs."

A skinny young man named Alex, who'd been involved in
anti-militia organizing in the area long before the issue made
it into the news, got up and invited questions. There were none
of substance from the reporters, but Joseph, who's an imposing
man even if he wasn't at that moment wearing his usual sidearm, spoke up from his spot in the back. "Here's a question,"
he said. "Have any of you spoken to the miners about this?"

Dave Strahan, no unimposing man himself, turned and bellowed, "I'm not here to answer your questions, Joseph!"

Joseph repeated himself and took several steps toward the
speakers. "So if I understand correctly," he said, "you haven't
spoken to the miners." It looked like there would have to be a
fight, with all the assembled news cameras rolling, but suddenly the speakers turned, as though by agreed-upon signal,
and fled in front of him into the courthouse. It later turned out
that they *had* agreed upon a retreat signal, in case it turned

out that things got threatening. The breakdown in the county couldn't have been more complete. Joseph stood outside the courthouse holding forth comfortably to the cameras, alongside a man who until a few months ago had been the county sheriff, Gil Gilbertson—who had come to support Joseph, not the people who'd just asked him to stand down. This was in a county with five working sheriff's deputies, to police eighty-five thousand residents. The Oath Keepers ruled the streets. Brandon Curtiss looked over to me and shrugged. "Where'd they go? You saw we didn't threaten anybody." This was true enough on the face of it, but there are some people—gangsters, riot cops, paramilitaries—who don't necessarily have to do anything other than show up and stand around to be threatening. And the Oath Keepers had made themselves those people.

The next day Mary invited us over to what she called a "staging area," a five-acre logistics base camp they'd set up on a very visible piece of property right up against the southbound lanes of Interstate 5 outside of town. We pulled down a short gravel road, and three guys in tactical gear holding rifles waved for us to stop and get out. They gave us looks sort of like what you'd give a couple of college boys you found at your daughter's slumber party and then went back to using a mirror, rudely fixed to a fir bough, to check under a waiting car for bombs. A lean and fit-looking man in his sixties with a pistol in a drop holster on his leg came out to escort us onto the base. He turned to Shawn. "There will be no taking of photos. Clear?"

This was partly an act. We passed the grim guardsmen, and as it began to rain again he turned back to Shawn. "That thing about the photos," he said, smiling the first smile we'd seen on the base. "Was it intimidating enough for you?"

He led us toward a rickety old trailer, where Mary had set up an office and a "media center," designated by a crude handwritten sign taped to the side. The staging area itself was a big gravel expanse, with a big camp kitchen and a few trailers and tents set up around a fire ring where guys were sitting around, smoking and talking. There were thirty or so cars in the lot, which meant there must have been quite a few people involved with the operation—most everyone had carpooled, some from thousands of miles away, none of the Idaho III% was there that day, and a lot of people were up at the mine or out running errands. Our escort led us to the trailer and took a position outside the door. We spent nearly an hour and a half inside, during which time the rain never stopped. "Nothing is going to happen," Mary said. "But in case something was going to happen, he's there. And you both know he's there. I think it's sweet."

The order of noncompliance was to come due the next day, and most of the volunteers seemed to be up at the mine, so we sat around and talked. Neil Wampler emerged to bring Mary a plate of fried potatoes. She thanked him, waited for him to leave, and tried a bite. She put them down. "He's a nice man," she said. "But he uses too much grease." She looked a little frayed. We tried to start talking, but her insurance agent called. She wearily told him she'd call back. "I had an accident coming down the hill the other day," she said. "A coyote ran in front of my car, and now all the guys call me Coyote Down." She said Joseph had lost fourteen pounds since things kicked off.

She'd come to Josephine County in 1989, following her

husband. "Back then you could hear it called 'the Beirut of Oregon,' " she told me. "I said, 'Where are you taking me?' " By coincidence this was at the beginning of the spotted owl crisis, when the inclusion of the northern spotted owl on the endangered species list eventually caused a federal judge to decide that BLM and Forest Service logging allowances threatened old-growth forests where the owls preferred to nest. He issued an injunction that essentially shut down the public lands logging industry in the Northwest, and an eventual compromise agreement still ended up limiting logging on federal lands to 20 percent of what they'd been before. Thousands of people lost jobs. Some might have lost them anyway, and the agreement saved old-growth habitat that could have never been replaced. But it hurt all the logging counties in western Oregon. It was a double hit: they lost jobs and the economies shrank, and they lost tax revenue from timber sales, which made it a struggle to pay for services and hit the economy even harder. Mary went to work for Sheriff Gilbertson as all of this was taking shape. He was a member of the Skousen acolyte Richard Mack's Constitutional Sheriffs and Peace Officers Association, a group devoted to the old and obscure segregationist canard that county sheriffs have the right to nullify federal law within their jurisdictions, something that has become one of the most potent forces in the constitutionalist coalition. County supremacy, as the legal theory is known, is as fundamental to the movement as the belief that the federal government doesn't have the right to own land, and to give an idea of their reach in 2016, the group was able to claim that the vast majority of sheriffs in the West—all but one in Utah, twenty-three out of thirty-six in Oregon—were members or supporters. It's hard to get elected in some places without being a member these days.

Citizens began forming vigilante groups to police themselves. The *New York Times* fretted in 2013 that "balkanized camps of armed residents could create new tensions" in the county. Gilbertson, even during a dark time when he had a single active deputy to police the whole county, still refused to support a tax levy to fund his department. Mary thought he was right. "It's not about us being antigovernment or anti–law enforcement," she said. "But people were saying, 'Give us these millions of dollars,' and it didn't add up."

She'd come to the Oath Keepers through the sheriff, and she got involved because they did volunteer work. "There was this project building a playground for disabled kids," she said. "Twelve of these guys came out, it was a hundred and three degrees, and then a wildfire started, so there was smoke they were breathing, and then it started to rain. And I remembered this one guy, an army ranger, he kept working—like, 'Well, at least it'll keep the temperature down.' Pretty much when there's an issue, they're the guys who stand up."

I liked her a lot. She was sweet to us and took it in stride that a twenty-eight-year-old with tattoos and long hair had flown out to follow her for a week. For her the Oath Keepers stood for neighbors and family and a comfortable, coherent way of life she'd known growing up, and I understood that feeling even if I didn't quite think she'd found the right vehicle. She reminded me, essentially, of my neighbors in Cincinnati—women who probably would have voted for John C. Calhoun if he was on the ballot, but who I could hardly see fit to judge, because they fed me, and took nights out of their lives to come to my piano recitals because it was the neighborly thing to do, and patched me up and cooed over me if I got knocked around in a fight and my mom wasn't around to deal with the situation.

Joseph sauntered in. "What are you talking to *these* guys for?" he asked, good-naturedly. He agreed, after something that approached begging on my part, to take us to the mine the next afternoon, the day the order was going to come due. I told him that I'd bought a topographical map and that I'd planned a way up, since I had to get a story one way or another. He looked slightly concerned for me. "Trust me," he said. "You wouldn't have made it very far."

We all went out to talk to the guys. "We're not toothless rednecks. We don't do the Aryan shit—that's the complete opposite of what we want," a young guy named Matt, from a group based in the Willamette Valley, sought me out to say. "That's not freedom. That's not equality. We've done classes on everything from small-animal butchering to sewing. We're just out to help each other out, help people out."

They were all also very resistant to the idea that they were antigovernment, and in fact we didn't meet a single person in any of the militias who would accept that term. At no point did anyone think to mention the name Barack Obama. A couple of guys from the Idaho III% pulled us over so that one of them, who made sure we knew he was Hispanic, could say to us, "Man, don't you write that we're antigovernment or anti-fed—we believe in government that people have a say in. We have Democrats. We even had a guy in the group who wanted to have, you know, a sex change. And there were some people who weren't okay with it. And we had a meeting and eventually some people had to leave." I asked who had had to leave. "The people who weren't okay with it!" he said. "We're constitutionalists, and what does the Constitution say about a sex change?"

The next day, Shawn and I loaded into Joseph's green Toyota Tacoma and drove up to the mine. "I don't believe they will come in here. I don't think that's in their best interest," Joseph said as we left the staging area. "But that being said, today is the deadline. For us it's a security operation, and whatever it takes to maintain the security of the mine is what we're going to do." He always talked like this.

He was intense to the degree that it was unnerving to share the cab of a pickup with him, but it was easy to see why scores of young military men who'd never met him before they drove in would follow him. He spoke with a firmness that made you think he wasn't used to being questioned back, but there was something earned about his self-assurance—he sometimes paused for half a minute while he searched for words, in the manner of someone who would rather say nothing at all than speak without first satisfying himself as to the justice of what he was saying. He grew up in the San Fernando Valley, in Los Angeles County, but moved to Massachusetts as a teenager. He joined the Massachusetts National Guard out of high school and flew both rotary and fixed-wing aircraft before bouncing around the country working in aviation, search-and-rescue, and fire suppression in Hawaii, Florida, Montana, and Alabama. Then he did three rounds as a contractor in Afghanistan, he says. He was injured in combat there and hasn't been able to work as a pilot since. "I broke my ankle in two places and blew out my knee. I got home Christmas Eve, got to the doc, and he said it was pretty well busted. It's been two years, and I'm still trying to get back to flight status."

He was also one of the pilots involved in the search for the Kim family, a story that became a statewide media sensation in Oregon after a family of four, heading to the coast during Thanksgiving vacation, followed a shortcut down a remote BLM road and became stranded in the snow. James Kim, the father, went for help but got lost and froze to death. Rice flew with a rescue operation for days and was one of the pilots who found his wife and kids, freezing by their car. Then he helped find James's body. He seemed to tear up when he told me this story, though I couldn't be sure. He still stayed in touch with James Kim's parents. Bear Camp Road, where they'd become lost, is now maybe the most famous stretch of BLM road in the country—it has its own Wikipedia page, at least. It also happened to be the road we turned down as we left the highway, heading into the woods.

I asked how he'd come to politics. "I was very distressed about what I had seen happen in this country after September eleventh," he said. "And I think that if what has happened to our rights and civil liberties since then had happened overnight, there would have been rioting in the streets.

"I've traveled a lot internationally," he went on, "and I can always tell the American, and it's embarrassing—because they're the only ones who reach down and take off their shoes at the airport. And when the government starts spying on

Americans and monitoring phone calls and keeping records on electronic traffic, and when you're keeping records on Americans just because they're Americans, and when you talk about warrantless wiretapping, when you talk about secret courts, when you talk about assassination of American citizens overseas without trial, that's not what I took an oath to defend."

I told him that I couldn't agree more. I found exchanges like this confusing and depressing, because on some level I couldn't help but be excited to meet people with whom I hadn't expected to agree on anything who shared my revulsion of the security state that had grown up in the Bush years, and I basically agreed with them that American lives had become too regulated and disconnected from any sense of community or belonging, and I didn't begrudge them their response to it. Bankers and debt pirates seemed like a much bigger threat to people I cared about than a few militiamen with guns. But they also never seemed to want to talk about corporate control of our politics, or prisons—a pretty big arm of the security state—and it was hard not to get the feeling that when things came down to it, all the things we agreed on would matter far less than a gut-level identification with the politics of the same reactionary billionaires who were so busily funding the drive to privatize public lands.

We pulled off the pavement and drove on through a beautiful woods, with an understory of madrone and a canopy of incense cedar. The radio came alive. "Break-break-break, all stations fire in the hole," someone said.

"They're blowing shit up," Joseph said. He wouldn't say

what they were blowing up, but it wasn't BLM trucks. All I could see were trees and forest. "Gook's going to blow his load!" the voice on the radio said. "Gook," it turned out, was the call sign for Brandon Rapolla, the guy who later set up my sleepover on the refuge.

We came to a bend in the road, where three guys with ARs stood next to a dozer that had been set up, flanked by at least one foxhole, dug in and hidden, making the road impassable.

"Hey, it's the boss!" someone called. They started the dozer, moved it off the road, and pulled it back into position when we'd passed.

We came to a huge clearing under shaggy hemlocks where Rick's cabin stood, proudly unburned. The tension, the waiting to see if something would happen, cleared as soon as we stepped out of the truck. It was a credit to Joseph that the guys in the operation had maintained a sense of discipline at all, because once up there it was impossible to imagine the BLM trying to send so much as a carrier pigeon up Bear Camp Road. The entrance to the mine was out of sight, up a steep one-lane track cut in the hillside. There were dozens of guys standing around, most of them armed and kitted out. It looked like they were massing to invade Yosemite. "And you can't even see most of the people who are up here," Brandon told us. Jason Patrick was there, chain-smoking, wearing his baggy suit jacket, and rushing around like always. Shawn and Brandon went off to do portraits in a patch of sun. "Get out of here, pretty boy," someone yelled. "Fuck off," Brandon yelled back. "I might get laid off of this." Soon other guys came over to get their pictures taken, and by the time I walked over, there were at least a dozen guys, all of them but Brandon younger than I was, most of them veterans.

And then a strange thing happened. I asked Brandon how these guys could get so riled up about the BLM but didn't seem to care much about banks running the country, or unarmed black men being shot by cops. Joseph would have given a politic answer, saying that he thought this was all part of a struggle for better government for everyone and things like that. But one of these kids piped up and said, "Well, you know, I think we'd like to." People nodded. "But we can't really, because we're the kind of people everyone thinks are rednecks and racists." I asked about Occupy Wall Street. "See, like, we would like to go to that," another guy said. "But I don't think they want us there." This was probably true. "And out where we live they do the same thing to those people as everyone does to us—like they just say they're homeless and unemployed and smelly hippies asking for a handout. Like I'd like to go learn about *them*, the way you guys are here talking to us. But you can't really do that in this country anymore." This got a big murmur of agreement. We stood there for a long time, and it became a tender and genuine moment—me shooting questions at them, guys volunteering earnest answers about how they felt hopeless and boxed out of politics and how they'd found friends up there at the mine like they'd never had back home.

There was a guy up there—call sign Grumpy—who had left his girlfriend and a newborn back home in Idaho, spent most of his savings on guns and gear, and come out without any clear idea of when he'd get back. I asked him if this wasn't maybe bizarre and unfair to his girlfriend, and he said she wanted him there. "I just think this is the most important thing I can do," he said. "To try to make sure my son grows up in a country with a constitutional government." They were in debt, mad at the banks, the bureaucrats, the people who looked down on them back home, and it felt hard to judge him. Jason was filming all this, and I'm glad he was, because I'm not sure it's a moment that would be possible to re-create now, at least not for me. We were all sort of pretending that we hadn't already picked sides.

We went up with Jason, Brandon, and Joseph to the mine itself. There wasn't much to see, unless you wanted to stoop and crawl in like the miners did, with a headlamp and a pick and shovel, and see how it extended for three levels carved wildly through the rock of the hill. I did not want to do this.

We drove out onto Forest Service land to see a miner who lived out in the woods, a sweet hippie type who told us a sad story about how a guy with a neighboring claim had threatened to kill him. He said he'd taken off to Oklahoma to hide out for a bit, and that when he'd come back he found that the Forest Service had burned his trailer and taken all his stuff. He showed us the burn site. Wild strawberries were coming up under broken glass and twisted bits of melted metal. We couldn't really prove that the Forest Service had done this extralegally, or that he ought to have had his trailer up there in the first place, but I didn't really think that was the point. It was sad either way.

On our last day there I went to meet up with Rick. "You have a GPS?" he asked when he set the meeting. I said I did. "Good," he said. "You can get lost like all the rest of the tourists."

He was a ball of muscle, even at fifty-eight. We shook hands. His fingernails, like those of all the miners we met, were as thick as nickels. I took a corner table at the general store—the only place of business of any kind near his house—in the tiny town of Applegate. I heard his story of growing up wandering the West while his father followed gas strikes—moving from Kansas to Texas to Utah and back—and how he'd come to Josephine County as a teenager and discovered mining. "We went up, the first time I did hard rock," he said, "and hell—there was gold just *laying* on the rocks."

We talked for a long time about the Oath Keepers and the BLM. He seemed oddly ambivalent about the whole thing. "There's lots of those folks who think that we should erupt into some kind of, I don't know what, guerrilla war," he said. "And that's very counterproductive. But they run people over all the time."

While we talked, a beautiful gray-haired woman, wearing elaborate jewelry and a linen dress, came up and introduced herself. He had clearly become a hero in town. "I just wanted to say good luck," she said. "I used to work the mines with my dad. Do you remember the Lost Blue Empress?" Rick said he did. She pressed his hand. "Keep it up."

We went out to his truck to look over some documents, and a guy in a flashy jacked-up Chevy pickup pulled up. "Can I have your autograph?" he asked saltily. "No, seriously, you're giving 'em hell, Rick." We all talked awhile, leaning on Rick's beat-up little brown truck and playing with his brown mutt, named Brown. "Brown's picture was in the *Daily Mail* of England!" he said in wonder. "Can you believe that shit?"

I said that it was he who'd brought on all the craziness in the first place. He admitted the truth of this, and I mentioned a video that had been made by Blaine Cooper, a moody wing nut who would end up being one of the core group at the Malheur standoff. In the video he was driving full-speed up toward the mine, talking about "heavy hitters" coming in and announcing grandly, "We can't let the Chinese or the government have the gold—it belongs to the people."

Rick gave a toothy smile. "Well, I don't know about that," he said. "The gold doesn't belong to the people. The gold belongs to me."

CHAPTER 13

Ammon

"Hey man, I like those boots." I looked up and saw Ammon's bodyguard, wearing truck-stop sunglasses, a camo ball cap, a camo jacket, and a little .38 revolver on his hip—the same getup he'd be seen wearing later that night in a clip on *The Late Show*. This sentence made up the first words spoken in what was to become maybe the oddest friendship of either of our lives. We were standing on the snowy access road right after the morning's press conference. The morning was gray but the cloud roof was so high that it was hard to call the weather anything but clear, and you could still see all the way across the basin. The boots were a cross between western riding boots and traditional work boots, made by Red Wing and slightly too big for me, and I've never been able to find a pair to replace them.

"Thanks, man," I said. I was heading up toward the parking lot to meet Shawn, who had just driven in from Portland.

"Back home they know me because I shotgun my boots," the guy said, and indicated the way his jeans were tucked into his own Ariat western-cum-work boots. "I'm a big boot guy."

I admitted that I held a lot of my net worth in boots, and

I told him about my three pairs of Luccheses and we got to talking about how I'd ended up there as much on a bizarre sightseeing trip as I'd come as a reporter. I mentioned that I'd been at the Sugar Pine and that the people who had been there mostly knew and trusted me, and he registered something in his eyes. "Hold on, I want to find someone," he said abruptly. "I'm Wes Kjar, by the way." He pronounced his last name "Care." Then he went off down the hill and I went up to the parking lot and found Shawn.

We had barely finished hugging and walking over from his silver Tacoma toward the watchtower and guard fire when one of the rotating cast of camo-clad men in balaclavas came and said, "Hey, are you James?" I said I was, and he said, "You want to come with me for a minute? I don't know what it's about, but I'm supposed to bring you to Ammon."

He showed us to the small stone office, where Wes was manning the door, past several reporters who had been standing outside hoping for admittance. Wes showed us in, and Ammon rose to greet us. He was wearing the same brown felt cowboy hat and blue plaid shirt jacket he wore through the whole standoff, and he was burly and bearded but improbably well proportioned for his bulk.

He shook our hands, said he'd heard about us, and, without explaining that comment, directed us to take a position at his desk, in the far corner of the room. Shawna Cox was there, sitting alert next to Ryan Bundy, who slouched in a swivel chair with a windbreaker, cowboy hat, and a revolver on his hip. Facing them was a family of ranchers arrayed in a semicircle, ranging from a redheaded little eleven-year-old in a

Stetson, boots, and a big belt buckle to what appeared to be his mother and father to a gravel-voiced and foulmouthed old man draped over a folding chair and wearing a giant hat. There was a whiteboard in front of them with diagrams and quotes from the Constitution. These were locals, some of the dozens who stopped by every day to talk to Ammon and receive his teachings. He'd wanted us to see the lesson.

It's hard to explain how surreal and thrilling this was. Everyone at the refuge treated Ammon like a prophet. His name—you could hear it on the radios, you could hear it in the way the more peripheral militia guys enunciated it—was like a passcode. Reporters at the press conferences received his smiles like benedictions, and then bragged over their whiskeys at the Pine Room next to the Days Inn about the solo access they'd gotten. He and his family were already well known to anyone who followed the standoff at the ranch in Nevada, and now the American politico-media complex had made him instantly one of the most famous people in the country, and maybe even briefly in the world—a sort of early avatar for all the divisions and insanity of 2016. Living on the refuge, it was easy to get a heightened sense of his magnetism. He'd summoned us to this tiny office with its ratty gray carpet and cheap swivel chairs and one overused toilet and a little kitchen good only for making coffee, and somehow the setting seemed far more intimate than even a one-on-one interview could have been. He smiled at us and took up a spot at the whiteboard. "So what we were saying," he said, "is, What's supposed to happen when two entities have a conflict?"

There was a pause. The boy pushed his hat back and looked

ready to say something. His mother nudged him encouragingly. "They're supposed to work it out themselves?" he said.

"Perfect," Ammon said, with infectious graciousness. "The Lord said, God said, you're supposed to love thy neighbor as thyself."

CHAPTER 14

A Brief Introduction to Bundyite Political Theory

I've heard Ammon give the lecture he was giving that afternoon so many times now that I could probably recite it by rote. He gave it every day on the refuge, to all the ranchers who visited to offer supplication or just to see the thing up close, and it was always astonishing how often even the skeptics came away convinced. One afternoon a guy named Buck Taylor asked for an audience, wanting to persuade him to take the show home. "That rancher is fucking tearing into him in there," someone told me when I asked what was going on. They talked for a while, and the next time I saw Taylor it was at a community meeting an hour away from the refuge in the tiny windswept village of Crane, where he was one of dozens of converts shouting down a guy with the temerity to question Ammon's vision of the Constitution. "I'm drinking the Kool-Aid," he told Oregon Public Broadcasting that night. "I haven't swallowed it, but I'm drinking it." People brought up Kool-Aid a lot, in reference to Ammon.

The effectiveness of the message is due to Ammon's delivery and to the fact that components of the message have been seeded throughout the rural West for generations. At the beginning of that meeting in Crane I heard Ammon quiz the crowd: "Who is the final arbiter of the Constitution?"

A lone, timid voice called out: "The Supreme Court?" There was an instant, angry, and honestly slightly disturbing chorus of nos and howls and boos from the assembled ranchers, which, even after years of seeing all this, frankly shocked me—this was damn near the entire adult male population of a strange town Ammon had never visited, where, if you believed the news reports, his ideas had no purchase, and yet these people seemed offended to the point of violence by the idea that the Supreme Court was responsible for interpreting the Constitution. "Right," Ammon said. "The people interpret it."

The Bundys, like W. Cleon Skousen before them, are Mormons who believe that the Constitution was inspired, if not more or less dictated wholesale, by God—and that the founding of the United States was the first step toward the restoration of Zion on the continent where most of the Book of Mormon takes place. But they've taken parts of the Skousenite philosophy and built their own system on top of it—as much a practical guide to living as a political schema, and it's something they teach as all their own, without citing any influences besides the Constitution and the Bible.

The Constitution, for the Bundys, is an expression of certain natural rights, which are basically our rights to life, liberty, and property, with a heavy emphasis on property. These are supposed to have been implanted by God and so natively obvious that all people sense them intrinsically. Property, for them, is gotten and maintained, in a very frontier way, by your right to "claim, use, and defend" it, as they repeat ad nauseam. It's a strange irony of the Bundys' ability to generate media attention that this is maybe the key trio of words in their entire ideology but that if you google "claim, use, defend" along with the name "Bundy," they seem to have not been able to get a single reporter to quote the phrase.

Ideal government, of which the Constitution is a more or less perfect expression, derives from the need to adjudicate between two parties claiming, using, or defending their rights or property when one or more isn't acting in good faith. He explained this theory of government in a perfect western vernacular.

"So say there's a conflict some people have, say over a fence. What are they supposed to do?" he asked that afternoon.

"I think you're supposed to talk it out," the little eleven-year-old said.

Ammon beamed. "Perfect! Did you hear that? The first thing we have is a right to work it out among each other. But let's say that there's someone that's hardheaded or that doesn't believe in God," he paused. "Or, I'm not saying that . . . but I think there's good people that . . ."

"They just get crosswised," the boy's mother said.

"Yeah," Ammon said. "Maybe I'm wrong by saying that. But anyway"—he paused thoughtfully—"let's just move on. So how do you resolve a situation where two people can't work it out amongst themselves?"

"They go to the court?" the boy said.

Right again. The states, in turn, existed to adjudicate intercounty disputes, and the federal government to deal with interstate. The logical follow-up to this was that if someone felt abused by their county government—rather than a citizen of the county—they could appeal to the state government, and suchwise for state and federal governments. "But now," he said, "what happens if you have a problem with the feds and you appeal?"

"Lose-lose?" said the mother.

"They go to the feds!" Ammon said. "They go to themselves. You know my dad says that going to federal court is like, a man walks into your house and he beats up your wife and children. And so you take him to court. And a man walks into the courtroom in a black robe and they say all rise for the honorable judge, and it's the very man that beat up your wife and children. The problem is that the federal government doesn't have the right to own rights," he said.

"Or land," Shawna, who was by Ammon's side almost constantly at the refuge, jumped in to say. "They can't own land."

"They do but it's very limited," Ammon said. "And the federal agencies don't have the right to own rights."

"What made them think they do?" the mother asked.

"They started it in about the turn of the century," he said, referring to the creation of the Forest Reserves and the Forest Service. "There's a whole history. But people didn't challenge it at that time."

"And now it's expanded," she said sadly.

"So look at what they've done to establish their rights around here. They claimed the land. They put their signs up and their logos on it. They restricted the use of it, saying now we're going to lease it back to you. And you know dang well that they're willing to defend it. The nice thing is that knowing all this makes it so easy to see how to fix it. And that's why we're here," he said.

"Welcome," the mother said.

"And so the solution is," he said, "we claim our rights, we use our rights, and we defend them."

Now came the stage where Ammon drew a map of the United States on the whiteboard. He then drew a box representing Washington, DC, which he invariably located somewhere on the latitude of Connecticut, and quoted selectively from the Constitution to say that the federal government was allowed to own only the "'ten miles square,' or actually that's a hundred square miles because ten by ten," of Washington, DC, along with "forts, dockyards, and other needful buildings" that could be built on lands ceded by the state. "The BLM thinks it owns 87 percent of Nevada," he said. "Is that a fort, dockyard, or other needful building?"

This argument is so compelling in its simplicity that it's hard to even talk it through with people who have heard it once. Because it seems to say it right there in Article 1, Section 8, Clause 17—that Congress shall have the right:

"To exercise exclusive Legislation in all Cases whatsoever, over such District (not exceeding ten Miles square) as may, by Cession of particular States, and the Acceptance of Congress, become the Seat of Government of the United States, and to exercise like Authority over all Places purchased by the Consent of the Legislature of the State in which the same shall be, for the Erection of Forts, Magazines, Arsenals, dock–Yards, and other needful Buildings."

It's hard to see how this would allow half the land in the West to fall under federal authority, and you could read this, if it was in your interest to do so, as restricting federal authority to precisely the places listed. But a fair-minded person could also read the intent of the clause as having to do with establishing a national capital and having basically nothing to do with the treatment of public lands thousands of miles away, which is how courts have always seen the matter. There are lots of things the Constitution doesn't specifically address—including, in this exact clause, the question of how Washington, DC, ought to be governed, since the exact text suggests that Congress ought to have the same authority over the city as it does over a military dockyard. And the Bundys conveniently never quote the Property Clause of Article 4, which is the article that was actually written to outline the relationship between the various layers of government, and which directly contradicts the whole point:

"The Congress shall have power to dispose of and make all needful Rules and Regulations respecting the Territory or other Property belonging to the United States; and nothing in this Constitution shall be so construed as to Prejudice any Claims of the United States, or of any particular State."

The Bundys are great defenders of the idea that anyone with passion and a pocket Constitution ought to be able to interpret the document and on this question, at least, that seems fair: "Nothing in this Constitution"—and one would have to think that this line applies to the bit that came before about the forts and dockyards as much as it does to anything else—"shall be so construed as to Prejudice any claims of the United States." The clause specifically articulates the government's right to regulate territories that have never fallen under the jurisdiction of states, and it specifically says that prior wording in the document, such as what the Bundys cite, shouldn't be misread to infringe on that right. It's not exactly complicated.

But in the Bundyite interpretation, the BLM and the Forest Service openly and merrily violated the Constitution in order to trample on westerners' property rights, which in their schema wasn't a small-bore range management question out on the fringe of the North American outback, but rather a violation and a mockery of a literally spiritual order of rights laid down in the Constitution, which itself was a mile marker on the road to Zion. The BLM was the family's particular obsession, but in theory it was sort of incidental—it just seemed to them like the biggest violator. Bert Smith, the outdoor store magnate, had spent his life and a large part of his fortune pushing this general idea—without it ever crossing over to a national discussion. But this is where the family's odd native political genius came in.

After the election of Barack Obama, groups like the Oath Keepers grew so quickly that they became hard to track or even to define—with the lines between militias and angry, beyond-the-fringe Republicans getting harder and harder to draw. Glenn Beck started promoting Skousenite philosophy on Fox News, and Skousen's book *The 5,000 Year Leap* quickly became the top seller on Amazon and stayed in the top fifteen for all of the fervid summer of 2009. Militias all over the country began calling themselves constitutionalists and seeing the Constitution as a sacred document as much as any Mormon.

For the most part, they were careful to avoid looking like the white supremacist militias of the 1990s, and for all their numbers they made little noise publicly. But when Cliven and Ammon linked the cause of ranchers and the rural way of life with the Patriot cause, it provided the movement a moral urgency it had lacked before, and also provided a neat trick for cryptoracists and white identity types. In Britain, it's very hard to talk about fighting for an "English way of life" without making it clear that some specific sorts of people aren't welcome in that vision of the country. But the Bundys took a picturesque, iconic version of an American way of life and made the argument that it was the purest representation of the way of life the Constitution, and God, had set down to follow. Patriot groups learned that you could preach cultural nationalism without ever really talking about anything but the Constitution. This trick has filtered up to Republican politicians across the country, which is why Republicans in state legislatures are always trying to ban Sharia law. They aren't anti-Muslim, of course, they just want to make sure we all follow the Constitution. This has made it very hard to say who, exactly, in all of this, is a racist. I personally don't think Ammon is nearly so animated by racial identity as most people on the left would assume—which isn't to say he doesn't feed and feed off of the same white tribalism that drove the 2016 election. It's just that he's so lost in his religious mission that he pretends race is not a motivating factor. But he has given space to genuinely hateful people like Jon Ritzheimer and Blaine Cooper, two of his lieutenants at the refuge, who like to do things like wear "Fuck Islam" T-shirts and make videos of themselves wrapping pages of the Koran in bacon and burning them. And there are some kinds of company you can't be forgiven for keeping.

The standoff united the ranchers and the Patriots who rallied to them in a family crusade to get more and more ranchers to refuse to pay grazing fees on public land—and eventually, by armed defiance, to break the entire land management system. From there they envisioned a whole reordering and deregulation of American life, and a rawhide-tinted vision of a West where public lands were held as a commons, with an overlapping system of claimed private rights working to let some people hunt, some people graze cattle, some people mine, all while sharing a good-old-days sort of open range.

LaVoy Finicum had been the first convert to the revolution, and he had decided to quit paying his grazing fees the day he met Cliven, on the first day of the Nevada standoff. Now they were looking for more. They didn't advertise that part at the press conferences, but they said it at their workshops with the ranchers. At the meeting in Crane, Buck Taylor, the jowly rancher who'd said he'd been drinking the Kool-Aid, stood up and asked Ammon what would happen if he joined the cause and the feds came to arrest him. Brian Cavalier, known as Booda, Cliven Bundy's giant, grizzled, ogre-looking body-guard, got up. He'd never met any of the Bundys when the standoff at the Nevada ranch popped off—he'd just driven up after leaving a job as a tattoo artist and a warrant for a bar fight back in Arizona. He'd ended up staying for two years, and now he was converting to Mormonism. "I was there when they came for Cliven," he told Taylor. "And if you stand with us, I'm going to be right there on your porch when they come for you, cowboy."

CHAPTER 15

Auras

"Every man radiates who he is," LaVoy Finicum told me once. "We can, in words and outward dress, try to conceal it. But sooner or later he reveals himself. The word is 'aura.' And when you become sensitive to that—pretty soon you can see who a person is." We were sitting in the cozy and quiet little room he'd made into an office, and we'd been talking for almost an hour, and I was nearly begging him to help me understand the strangest emotional reality of the standoff, which was that certain people, who were mostly Mormons but who weren't all Mormons, became trusted and even intimate with Ammon and his inner circle much faster than you would think was possible for anyone by the normal human modes of conversation and watching people go through the world. In turn, the sudden devotion of people to the person of Ammon struck me first as sort of funny and improbable, and then, by the end, as something twisted and dark.

Wes, the bodyguard, had clearly been reading auras and had had his read, because he'd showed up only a couple of days before me. LaVoy had vetted him. He'd been raised Mormon and he was from Manti, Utah, down in the part of the state where the western insurrectionist movement has always been at its strongest, but he'd stopped going to church. He was thirty-one, he'd recently discovered drinking, and he was making good money on oil rigs out in North Dakota. He had a brand-new Jeep and a five-ton military truck he used for off-roading and showing off to the girls, and he'd been a state wrestling champ. It was hard to see what he was doing there. "People back east, man, they don't understand this shit with the BLM. For us out here it's like our whole lives," he told me. "And I just thought that if here he is finally making a stand I would make a stand with him." He'd come alone, driving the Jeep from North Dakota with an AR and no exact plan. In this sense he was following the same pattern of LaVoy, Blaine Cooper, Booda, and Ryan Payne—of the ten or so people in the inner circle of the occupation, half of them had never met anyone in the family before they'd showed up in Nevada and pledged their "lives, fortunes, and sacred honor," as Jason Patrick had quoted to me, to the family's cause.

"I don't know any tactical shit," he told me. "I'm just a country boy with a sidearm. And I told myself at the very beginning—do not point a gun at a federal officer. But they said, 'Will you catch a bullet for Ammon?' and I said sure—I can be a bullet catcher." He'd barely even met the man.

That afternoon, after the workshop with the ranchers, Shawn took pictures, and Wes brought me to Ammon and Ryan. We spoke for a minute, and something happened that, ever since, I've had a lot of trouble trying to explain. We were standing around the little office, Ammon standing a bit taller than me and sort of looming, and a strange glow of cheer seemed to suffuse the whole place, which was too small for the traffic it got during those weeks and, with its stone walls, was constantly humid and clammy, the carpet stained, the tramp of heavy men in heavy boots and the butts of rifles always thudding on the floor. The catalyst was Ammon's good mood. He had a weakness, I was to notice, for foreign journalists, and he invited in two French TV reporters and a skinny English Reuters staffer named Jonathan Allen, who was taking a break from the Hillary campaign. The room took on a character of a tea social, with the French TV guys looking bewildered and Shawn wandering around shooting photos and Wes, Ammon, Ryan, Jonathan, and me standing in what in most situations would have seemed like oddly close proximity to one another while Ammon and I talked about his family, his job, Mormonism, and what it was like to live in New York. His sixth child, a boy named Elias, was just two days away from his first birthday. I expressed some shock that he was going to be away. "Well, we felt like we had to be here," he said. "So I miss them, it's horrible."

"Do you Facetime with them?" Jonathan asked.

"Skype," Ammon said.

I said my feeling was that the only thing that would heal the western insurgent mind-set at this point was if ranchers and environmentalists learned to talk to each other about land management issues, and he surprised me by saying, "I agree," in a way that I found earnest and believable. I said that I thought the biggest impediment to that was the movement by corporate-funded enablers to transfer land back to the states, which would destroy multiple use as we knew it in this country. You couldn't really expect environmentalists to meet in the middle when this was the premise of the discussion. He cut me off.

"There are plans, like say in Utah, to transfer federal land to the state. We oppose that as much as any other plan!"

I expressed disbelief. I hadn't yet fully understood that they might want something different than the corporate state-transfer advocates, and I found the notion disarming.

"No, we're against that movement," Ryan said. "Then the state becomes the new master."

"They established the West on multiple use. So on a hundred-acre parcel the rancher can own the grazing rights. But it has to be for the people—campers can camp, fishers can fish, hunters can hunt . . ."

"But now the BLM is even making you get a camping permit," Ryan said.

"I know, I do hate that."

"Well see, you ask a good question, and this affects you too," he said.

Some militia guys called over the radio. They were looking for Shawn and me, concerned that we'd overstayed our welcome. Ammon looked annoyed. "No, don't let them interrupt this," he said.

"He's with us," Wes said over the radio. This was the final word. It was only long after the standoff, talking to Shawna, that I learned they'd got together and assessed my aura too. Whatever it was I was radiating that day passed the test, and we were all grand friends by this time—no one was drinking so much as coffee, but it felt sort of like that golden last half hour before saying good-bye after a big night of revelry with new friends, and it had all developed so quickly that I sort of forgot to be surprised or to wonder if I was somehow in danger of being compromised. Ammon and I posed for a picture that makes me strangely uncomfortable to look at now, both of us in cowboy hats with our arms around each other, big dumb grins on our faces. Ammon slipped off to confer with Wes and then called us over. He asked if I had a car. I said I did. "Okay," he said, in a low, conspiratorial whisper. "So you know how it's Elias's birthday on Friday? I want to sneak out of here and surprise the family. And I was thinking you could drive me, so no one will know. We'll spend the night at my house, eat dinner with the family, and come back in the morning." He invited Jonathan and the French TV guys along too. Jonathan, sensibly, declined. The rest of us jumped. "Clean out your car," Wes told me, "and be ready when I call."

CHAPTER 16

Revolutionary Politics

"Come on outside," Joseph Rice said by way of greeting, "where I can throat-punch you for real." He was mad about the nakedly sensationalist subtitle that had been given to the piece I did about the Sugar Pine. "And dude, what's with your cowboy hat?"

Joseph and most of the guys from the Sugar Pine had shown up, in force, in the day since we'd been introduced to Ammon—an influx that had, almost instantly, transformed the county into a place that felt like it was in the grip of a full-scale revolution. The Oath Keepers' national organization had split, and the remaining gang of authoritarian law-enforcement types were busily eradicating the civil libertarianism and political ecumenism that I'd seen—and to some degree found endearing—from the guys at the Sugar Pine. I'd been right to wonder how genuine our coming-together had been—Joseph had already thrown himself into electoral politics, and he ended up going to Cleveland as a Trump delegate to the Republican National Convention. It's pretty hard to square this with what he told me about being horrified by the War on Terror.

But Joseph and Brandon Rapolla—the giant Guamanian

head of security at the mine who had gone by Gook—and the guys from the Idaho III% had split off from the Oath Keepers and made a reconstituted umbrella group, called the Pacific Patriots Network. They'd rolled into Burns and set up armed foot patrols in the middle of town. They made huge demonstrations to warn the FBI of what would happen if they moved on the refuge. Now, to see them parading in convoys of dozens after dozens of trucks flying flags, ARs showing through the windows, honking and moving at a deliberate, military pace past the refuge or around town, where they brought their demonstrations to all the points of power—to the courthouse, to the FBI base at the airport—I kept thinking that it looked like a guerrilla convoy in some riven republic, and then catching myself and remembering that in a literal sense that's exactly what I was looking at.

If they were practicing revolutionary politics, the commissars at the vanguard were locals who had been formed, with Ammon's help, into a group called the Harney County Committee of Safety. This was a name borrowed from various rebel councils set up prior to the American Revolution, and the idea, then as now in Oregon, was to establish a temporary shadow government to act as a sort of revolutionary junta working in defiance of a tyrannous government that had lost its legitimacy. The crank constitutional scholars whose ideas had so effectively influenced the Bundy family and so many other westerners had been pushing the idea of the committees of safety as something that, because it had happened in the Revolution, was part of a living American political tradition—that counties had a right to form these committees and to expect their demands to be heard. The committee had submitted a "Redress of Grievances" to the sheriff and the county commissioners, demanding the return "to the people" of federal lands in the county, and took it as an affront to republican principle that it hadn't been acted upon. No one had actually voted on this, which was less of a problem than you might think; one of the early lessons taught in the fringe constitutional movement is that the United States is a "republic, not a democracy," where "men of initiative"—like the founders, or like Ammon—have as much right to make policy as voters. The county fire chief had been on the committee since it was formed, and when the county commissioners asked him to withdraw he refused, and instead he held a press conference, standing next to Ammon, at the refuge. "I've been told that we don't know what we're doing," he told the cameras. "I've been told that my life is in danger. I've been told all kinds of things. I will not be told what to do." Then he announced he was resigning as fire chief.

Now, the day that the PPN had shown up, the junta was having a meeting, and it had brought land rights activists and militia members from across the West. The reconstituted Oath Keepers sent their new communications director, a chubby guy from Montana in a cowboy hat. Brandon Curtiss, the head of the Idaho III%, was there, and he wrapped me in a big hug when he saw me. He's since gone bankrupt, amid accusations of fraud and nonpayment at his real estate management business, and was then arrested and charged with aggravated assault after he allegedly put his hand on his holster and threatened to kill a woman trying to serve him papers in a lawsuit over the nonpayments, all of which was excitedly documented for the public by the *Idaho Statesman*. E. J. Parker, the I-15 sniper from the Nevada standoff, was there. He shook our hands warmly and said it was good to see us.

The meeting was held at the senior center, and the room was packed and electric, which was now seeming like the norm for things like this. The main spokesman for the committee was a lumbering old rancher named Tim Smith, whom I'd first seen at the sheriff's community meeting. He always wore a big white cowboy hat and was such a terribly awkward, halting public speaker that I always found myself rooting for him to carry off his speeches just because I felt sorry for him. But no one else seemed to mind much, and they kept throwing him up to stumble in front of the national media.

We found Joseph after the speeches. He was wearing a white ball cap and a white T-shirt and looked fresh and in charge. We defused the throat-punching thing by saying we hadn't had any control over that part, and he said, "Well, you repaid us already." I asked what he meant, and he said, "We've been in touch with Ammon about you already—why do you think you got let on the refuge that night? We called the FBI and told them we had a journalist on there." Now I wanted to throat-punch him, because until then I hadn't been fully aware of how deliberately they'd set me up for their own purposes that night. He shrugged and made an all's-fair-in-love-and-war kind of face.

I stalked away without exactly figuring out how to express how angry I was. "This is fucked," I said to Shawn. "I mean, yeah," he said. He was unfazed. It was hard to faze Shawn.

"But everything about all of this has always been fucked, though."

I had already greeted Brandon Rapolla, who had rolled into the refuge in his big blue Ram diesel, with what looked like supplies to survive two world wars in the bed, and within minutes was walking around like he owned the place. "I was pissed, man," he told me. "Our rule has always been that we engage in defensive actions. We don't do offense, taking over buildings, endangering lives, things like that. But you know Ammon: he does things his way. And now here we both are, huh?" We fist bumped, and he went off to lead a parade of pickup trucks of armed men through a quiet American town.

CHAPTER 17

Landscape of Rebellion II

Even today people tend to lump all this western ferment under the label of the Sagebrush Rebellion, which makes sense, because even outside the technical bounds of the Great Basin the ferment is strongest where the sagebrush grows. Its Latin name, *Artemisia tridentata*, comes from the fact that each of its tiny, silver-gray leaves is divided into three elongated lobes, each ending in a little "tooth." The teeth are more pronounced in healthier plants. The leaves have a soft, furry aspect that you notice if you look closely, and they're usually evergreen, though, like many desert plants, they'll sometimes drop leaves in the summer to reduce stress and water loss. Living in a so-called cold desert, where the summers are brutal and the winters are just as bad, has made it very flexible. It'll grow far outside the confines of its homeland, and you can see its various forms on rocky slopes ten thousand feet high on the western slope of the Sierra, on the steppes of Wyoming, and down into the Baja Peninsula. When I was twenty-five, very lonely, and obsessed with the botany of the West, I acquired some little basin sagebrush plants and put them in a corner of my garden in Los Angeles. I had an overhanging tree and very little space and had to put them in a spot that got

only three hours of good sunlight a day, even in summer. A bota-
nist I mentioned this to told me the plants would be dead within
a month. Three weeks after that conversation they were putting
on growth, and after three more weeks they were ready for sex,
producing tiny yellow flowers, each producing a single tiny seed.
All sagebrushes pollinate by wind. Outside its normal range the
plant guards its forces and stays small, sometimes so small you
could crush it with a step, and high in the mountains they
seem to huddle around that size for years. But on a basin floor it
can grow from a single gnarled, woody stem into a huge bush,
taller than a man and spreading even wider. Westerners call it
"big sagebrush."

When a plant feels particularly happy and the sun is shin-
ing, the narrow leaves will stand up so stiff and erect they seem
to quiver with potential energy, and the plant will release aro-
matic oils that smell sort of like sage, but subtler and much
more astringent. You can crush the leaves in your fingers to
smell it too, but this activates the astringency and ruins it for
some people. The sage-like smell is why it's called sagebrush,
but real sages, including the herb used for cooking or the white
sage you might buy as a bundle to burn in your new apartment,
are members of the genus *Salvia*, in the mint family. They have
bigger leaves, sweeter smells, and a more delicate constitution
than the sagebrushes. They quiver with excitement and give
off their scent when they're happy too—but they're sort of
meretricious about it, leaking sickly sweet oil you can smell
from yards away and that rubs off on your fingers and mixes
with your sweat and leaves you smelling and feeling like
you've just made out with a hippie. They grow very fast, and

their heavy oil content makes them explode like bombs when a fire rolls through. Sagebrush burns almost as fast, but hotter and longer, and you can make a good campfire out of the green wood.

The wood of most western conifers burns quickly and leaves so little coal that it's hard to cook on or to build into a fire to keep you going through a cold night, and across the Great Basin, from Oregon down to Arizona, you'll mostly find trees only at the higher and colder elevations. It was often sagebrush that kept travelers crossing the northern desert alive. The smoke keeps away mosquitoes, and the leaves can be used to preserve food and keep away rodents. Hiding under a lone bush, or screened within thick stands of it, you'll find the sage grouse, sage rats, which are like a cross between a prairie dog and a subway rat, snakes, coyotes, quail, jackrabbits, and cottontails, and along the railroad tracks and back roads and outskirts of cities you'll find it giving cover to sleeping hitchhikers and trainhoppers and old homeless drunks. Cows, elk, and deer are thought to dislike the taste of sagebrush, and the accumulation of the bitter oils in their bellies can give them a stomachache. This is a protective mechanism; the oil content of the plants is highest in spring, to reduce grazing as the plants come into flower. But in winter the oil content drops and the seedheads become important winter forage. The plants talk through the oils too: when one sagebrush does get browsed by an herbivore with an adventurous palette, the injured plant releases a scented plume, as a sign to the neighbors to up their own defenses by increasing oil production. It's my favorite plant, and one of the things that pisses me off most about the framing of the so-

called Sagebrush Rebellion is the implication that the plant
and the places where it grows belong somehow to a tribal
grouping of people who I very much doubt care more or have
any deeper connection to the plant than I do.

CHAPTER 18

Outlaw State of Mind

The next day Wes called my phone before nine, while I was still in the bath at the motel and far from having dealt with the hangover I'd acquired at the Pine Room the night before. Shawn and I were becoming friendly with Bill, the wiry owner, who had a severe buzz cut and a quiet but extremely curt demeanor toward his staff, and to some degree toward me when he found me drunk and loud, which was often. He liked Shawn much more, and was always trying to persuade him to buy property in the area. "Look at this place," he'd say. "Got it for forty thousand dollars, rented it in two weeks, after ten grand of work. Rental market here is huge because ranchers move into Burns and need to live somewhere, don't they? Twelve percent return on investment. You know many investments that'll beat that rate of return?" We certainly did not.

He had worked for the BLM for decades but was slightly coy with his opinions on the standoff at the refuge or about the guys from the PPN stalking around town. He was doing three times his usual winter business. It turned out that many of the people who had turned out to support the occupation drank beer and ate T-bones just like the locals. And anyway it didn't exactly pay—in Burns or anywhere else in the rural West—for a publican to take too hard an opinion one way or another on a protest against the federal government. He'd just retired from federal service and he was getting ready, when everything cooled down, to live out an old dream of going for a big-game hunt in Namibia. This really did end up happening—I know because months later he showed me the pictures, printed out and numerous. He went alone, killed a lot of kudu, and looked very happy.

"Can you get down here quick?" Wes asked me. "I want to talk about, you know, the trip out of here, but not on the phone. Just come straight to Ammon's office. The guys know you have access there now."

I ate half an Adderall and drove the thirty miles at a hundred miles an hour, with apologies to the tires and transfer case on my sister's Highlander. I'd been in such a low, lost place before I came out—traveling constantly back and forth to and from Cincinnati, to help my mom and spend time with Jen, and then to be with the family after Reppie died, and obsessing about what was going to become of us had become sort of my main job, not that I had very much to offer. I was spending a lot of time in bed taking drugs and worrying about my family, which seems defensible, and also freaking out about my life in a typical twentysomething-in-the-city sort of way, wondering if I wanted to keep writing, and taking more drugs, which is maybe less so.

Then you add that I was not at all immune to the mechanics of American media churn and instant celebrity obsession—which had done its quick work building Ammon into a political and cultural polestar, even though almost everyone I knew who wasn't one of my strange militia acquaintances loathed and reviled him. I understood very crassly that proximity to him, and the sudden interest he seemed to take in me—an interest that I knew even then was probably halfway just in my head, but whatever—had given me both an emotional jolt out of my druggy somnolence and a project to get me out of bed in the morning, and I found myself desperately attached to both. And, hence, to deepening my interaction with whatever this movement was.

I'm not sure how much of this Ammon sensed or cared at all about, but he sensed some of it, and he knew that I needed him more than he needed me and he had an idea of how that could be useful. By this time the *New York Times Magazine* had already given me the go-ahead to say I was working for it on a big story about this thing, which was the sort of journalism I never exactly envisioned myself doing but was helplessly exciting in the moment, and it gave Ammon, now dealing every day up close and personal with someone from the *Times* with whom he could really get down and who had hung out in the West—not one of these fly-ins who came to write eight-hundred-word pieces that, as he saw it, were all environmental movement propaganda—a strong incentive to work on me the same charisma and/or crazy supernatural mind powers that he used on all these other youngish men who had come to him and been enraptured.

I had spent the day previous with Wes, hoping against hope that the trip to Idaho would come together. It would have been a great magazine narrative, and I badly needed a win. Brandon Rapolla was the main voice against it. "Dude, I mean, you see all these 'UPS' trucks passing by the refuge?" he said. "You think they're delivering packages thirty miles from the nearest town?" I wasn't exactly sure, since, unbelievably, the sanitation guys were still coming to pick up the trash, and the mail came as normal and the lights were all still on, but I took his point. "They're gonna take you guys down as soon as you cross the county line," he said.

The PPN were all around when I got there. I said hi to a guy named Hollywood, so called because he's a gaunt white guy with a scraggly blond beard and a dead-eyed scowl who looks pretty scary when he stalks around with a rifle, and since he joined the Idaho III%, photographers have always rushed to take his picture. The demeanor of the place had changed somewhat when the PPN got there—outside of the guards at the gates I hadn't seen many long guns around, and in the daytimes it had been mostly local ranchers, reporters, and sage hens wandering around. Now it felt much more serious. I went into the office and, somewhat to my shock, found that Ammon's entire family was already there, from his busy, serious, thirty-six-year-old wife, Lisa, all the way down to baby Elias. They had come in secret in a big red Expedition with a "Bye Bye BLM" bumper sticker on the back. I was very disappointed, realizing that this meant my big narrative adventure of ferrying Ammon out of the standoff was sunk, but Wes called me over and asked me to come upstairs with him, to the little attic room where he and Ammon had been sleeping next to each other on thin mats on the floor, next to an AR propped against the wall and a big black taxidermied crow that they'd moved upstairs because it kept creeping people out.

"So I've been thinking," he said. "Like, we want to show that this isn't a siege, that people can come and go and there isn't going to be a shoot-out at the perimeter if they do. And you know now I'm one of the central figures somehow, and my picture's on TV and stuff." I nodded. "And like I figure if I go out we might be able to establish that Ammon could go out safely, and if that happens then like maybe he can even go home . . . or something like that, I don't know." He cut himself off abruptly, switching back to a species of bravado.

"So I was thinking that I have some guns and money that I want to get down in Salt Lake City," he said. "And I gotta get the permanent tags for my new Jeep, because I came out here without dealing with that." Then the bravado broke again. "And, I don't know, man," he said, taking off his camo ball cap for the first time I'd seen, and showing his bald head and worried face. "I don't, like, I mean—man, you don't know what the stress of being around Ammon constantly is. Drones and stuff and thinking about going to jail and . . . Like I was thinking we could spend the night in Salt Lake, go country dancing, drink some beers, meet some girls—just unwind a little before we come back here with all the paranoia and shit." He had profiled me as someone that this sort of itinerary would appeal to, which wasn't exactly misplaced.

I said I was open to the idea. "So you want to load up your car and we can leave this afternoon? And then, you know, if they do take us down and arrest me, you can witness it and get a story?"

"Dude," I said, "I'm happy to go and you can do what you want to do, but I can't drive you if you're going to, like, get guns. Or anything at all that helps this thing." I wasn't exactly sure where the line of propriety was.

"Okay, hold up," he said, only momentarily deterred, he said. "Let me find us a ride."

I texted my editor at the *Times*, because I was confused as to whether this was a ridiculous or unethical plan. He said that he thought I ought to figure out a way to go, so I shrugged and went and hung out with Ammon's family for the afternoon— letting baby Elias drool on my phone while he gnawed on a beef stick from a package labeled Eastern Oregon Mobile Slaughter, and chatting with his oldest boy, Hadley, about foot- ball. He was a linebacker. I said he seemed a bit skinny for that. "That's what my mom says," he said. I said he'd grow into it. "They won't let me wrestle yet," he said, and I said it was a shame but that I was sure he'd do fine when he did. He wore a crisp cream cowboy hat and seemed extremely mature for his thirteen years.

Everyone was in a good mood. They kept bringing up memes that had been used to make fun of them all in the lib- eral corners of Twitter. "What was the one?" Blaine Cooper asked. "Vanilla ISIS?" There was a roar of laughter.

"And we're Y'all Qaeda," Wes said. "Doing . . . what was it again?"

"Yeehad," I said. Even Ammon laughed. Wes had seen him- self on *Colbert*, in a picture that featured him and Ryan Payne.

"I haven't seen this many angry bearded men in Oregon since I called Blue Moon a craft beer," the first punch line went. He then proposed that the government let the occupiers have the refuge, and rename it the Ammon Bundy Preserve for the Armed and Cranky. "They're clearly endangered," he said, putting up a picture of Ammon standing between Wes and Blaine Cooper, both wearing camouflage. "Though it's hard to know how many there are, because their camo is so good—here's Ammon Bundy standing between what I believe are two bushes." Wes recounted this, and the room went wild.

I asked Lisa if it was bizarre to see Wes, whom she'd never met, serving as her husband's bodyguard and shadow. She was dark-haired, pretty, and much less harried than you'd think a mother of six watching her flock at a federal standoff would be. It was almost impossible to reconcile this picture of her with the haunted woman she'd look like a few weeks later, in videos relaying Ammon's messages from jail. "I don't care about their backgrounds," she said. "If they're willing to give their life, then I trust them." These are maybe not the same grounds on which everyone I know judges a spouse's friends, but all marriages are unique. "I was going to come out just myself to get a feel for it," she said. "But Ammon said, 'No, I need to see my family.' And of course I trust him."

It was getting into the late afternoon. The baby had somehow acquired a chocolate lollipop and walked around jabbing it at his mouth, getting chocolate on the furniture and his face in the process. "Mom!" Hadley said. "He's going to get a sugar rush again."

"Okay then! Break it in half," she said and rolled her eyes

at me. We laughed. Behind her Wes was talking to Ammon. He shook his hand and said, "We're just going to show it's not a standoff, that we can leave and come back. I'm not done here." Ammon watched him sadly. He was very sensitive to emotional currents, and it was obvious, watching his face, that he was skeptical of the idea that this was just a supply run. When our eyes met, his eyebrows were slightly raised. We waved, and Wes motioned to me. "We've got a ride, bud," he said. "You ready?" I had nothing with me really but my phone and a pack of cigarettes, but I said sure. "Meet me in the white Expedition," he said.

CHAPTER 19

The Central Pastime

I went outside and found a gigantic, custom, six-door stretch limousine 4x4 Expedition idling. There seemed to be nothing to do but get in, so I climbed aboard and found myself surrounded by three middle-aged men I'd seen once or twice around the refuge but hadn't met. They regarded me with naked wariness. The one driving, a long, lean, dark-bearded man in a black cowboy hat, barely looked at me at all, just pulled his hat down to the point where it almost entirely covered his eyes, leaned his seat back, pulled the collar of his shearling jacket up around his throat, and drove out of the lot. Wes rolled down the window as we passed the men at the campfire checkpoint. He was full of bravado again. "I've got a few more ARs I can get," he said. "And just let me know if you want any tac gear. Tell Ammon or something and he can text me."

It was snowing by the time we got to Burns, where we were to pull onto the highway to head toward Idaho and Utah. I still hadn't been able to figure out who the men were, exactly. They wanted to stop for dinner, since it would be hours before we hit the next town, and so we went to the Central Pastime, which is maybe the only weird rural dive bar I've ever been to that I genuinely hate. It has inedible food and caters to a rougher and more antigovernment element than the Pine Room. This makes it interesting, but the place is garishly lit and the music is always either eerily quiet or way too loud and there's a surly feel about it that makes it hard to pick up a conversation with a stranger. "I honestly don't like it when I can't see a gun on a guy in here," one of the bartenders, a cranky thirtysomething woman, said to me once. "It means it's concealed, and then you don't know where you stand. Or that he doesn't have one, which I don't like either." I saw her a lot over the next year, but she never once seemed to remember me.

Some of the PPN guys were there, and I had a vodka at the bar with Hollywood. "Give me the worst vodka you have," he told the bartender. "That way I'll taste it." I followed him. "Round two," he said, raising the glass immediately after downing the first. I followed him. "You know," he said, "this stuff is politics or whatever, but I don't really think of it that way. We do stuff, we go places, we meet interesting people. I mean, here you and I are, right? How else would we have met? I'm not saying it's a social club, but it's kind of a fucking social club. And these are my brothers." He seemed—all the PPN seemed, actually—slightly perturbed by the heavy feel at the refuge, the sense that, unlike at the Bundy ranch and the Sugar Pine mine, there was no deliverable victory to win. Ammon was talking about staying for "years."

The Obama administration was not going to pardon the Hammonds to appease his messianic demands, and Ammon was smart and politically astute enough to know this, even if he pretended otherwise at his press conferences. The occupiers had committed offenses that were obviously worthy of arrest—trespassing, bringing firearms into a federal facility. If they didn't leave—and, like, leave *pronto*—the government was going to have to act on those offenses out of the simple mechanisms of political pressure and a need to restore something like the appearance of rule of law in the West, because at this point it was not at all hyperbolic to say that it had ceased to exist. And from people in the environmental movement to the governor of Oregon, too many close and important Obama supporters were too angry about the occupation for the Justice Department to let this slide, even if there had been an inclination to do so. The occupiers had already said that they would resist arrest by force. The ultimate logic of these facts was either that Ammon was going to succeed in starting his revolution or that people were going to die and go to jail for a long time. Ammon knew all of this. There was no going back, and that was the whole point. I felt ill, though that was partly attributable to the gelatinous steak sandwich on margarine-soaked Texas toast that I had just tried to force down. The time for social clubs was done. Hollywood got that.

Brandon Rapolla flagged me, and I went over to his table. Brooke, the tiny, dark, and fierce-looking woman who served as the sort of first lieutenant of the Idaho III%, was laying down the rules for their patrols through town. "We're not doing long guns in public," she said. "You can open carry sidearms, but leave the rifles in your rigs. And you all need to double-check to see if your conceal carry licenses have reciprocity for Oregon—if not, then you're definitely going to open carry."

The Bengals were playing on TV, so Brandon and I watched that and drank a beer. He was openly worried about someone getting killed. That afternoon, amid the family visit and all the levity, someone in the tower had given a "To Arms" call over the radio. Wes, handling the radio for Ammon, had paused for a minute, and then done as he'd been instructed, which was to take every such call as the gospel truth, and so he'd relayed it to the office with a shout, at which point the place became a nest of guns and Brandon had come thundering down the attic stairs, his huge, improbably spry, and poised bulk decked out in tactical gear and seeming to take up the entire office. There was a brief moment where it looked like it was going to be on. He was livid when he'd found out that the call had come from guys joking around in the watchtower, having made it after seeing a minivan full of women rolling in past the men by the fire at the gate. He was getting out before shit got bad.

"You know people out east and people in politics and stuff," he said. "What do you think makes them go in there?" I said that I thought the FBI had no real incentive to try to storm the place until pressure from Oregon officials on the Justice Department and the White House became too great for continued inaction, and that then I thought anything at all could happen. He nodded and sipped, brooding. "Where are you off to?" he asked. "You want me to tell you?" I said. "No, good point," he said, laughing. "You're learning OPSEC! Good luck, though."

We drove out of town in a snowstorm with the four-wheel-drive engaged, and within what seemed like minutes we were climbing into the improbably named Stinkingwater Mountains toward Idaho. We had rearranged our seats, and now the laconic dark cowboy, who turned out in fact to be a former saddle-bronc rider named Jon Pratt, occupied a bench seat in the back. The truck was amazingly big. Wes had a bench to himself in front of Jon, and I had one behind the front seats, where a wiry and manic wisp of a man named Steve Maxfield had taken over driving. Next to him there was a genial, slow-talking, and sturdy lawyer named Todd MacFarlane, who was the one who'd taken it upon himself to explain who they all were.

They were all Mormons from the tiny town of Kanosh, down in southern Utah—which is the kind of place where it seems like everyone knows at least a cousin of everyone else, no matter how many hours by two-lane highway away their little towns are from each other. They'd come up at Steve's instigation, because Steve had seen LaVoy doing the interview where he said all the stuff about dying before he'd go to jail. Steve, who did crazy, $200,000 custom-truck builds with sky-high-lift kits and extended chassis with extra doors and things like rear-wheel steering for tight cornering while off-roading, had got it in his head that they could come up and talk some sense into LaVoy. "I'm a doer," he told me within minutes. He talked amazingly fast. "I put stuff together. And I put this together."

"That's true, he did," Todd said. "You do put things together, Steve." Todd and Jon had been at the Bundy ranch, but in their telling mostly just to see it. They all knew one another from what they called the Liberty Movement, and Todd, at least, was a friend of and close collaborator with Bert Smith. Steve had persuaded Todd to come along, and Todd had persuaded Jon. They had loaded up the limousine Expedition, which was one of Steve's custom creations, and headed up. Jon did not seem to like Steve very much, but then Jon did not seem to like anyone very much. He lay in the back and spoke not a word for the first two hours. Wes had linked up with all of them because Todd was originally from down around Manti and knew his father. They were going to drive us down to Salt Lake City, where Wes would get his supplies and money and from there figure out a car back. Steve turned to me and began to talk very quickly about how they were okay with having me along, "but we don't know you, and we're going to have to feel out where you're coming from." He and Todd explained in the sternest possible terms that everything that happened on the trip was to be off the record, which was an order they thankfully ended up rescinding.

Steve pointed out a fence that had been edging the road for a ways. "Nice fence over there," he said to Todd.

"Yeah," Todd said. "Nice."

I failed to suppress a laugh. Todd turned to ask what was funny. I said I thought it was funny how you could always tell a westerner by the way that, no matter how far afield they traveled, they were always checking out fences, making fun of run-down ones, drooling over nice ones. There was a weird pause. Then they both laughed. "You got us on that one," Todd said. "We do love fences." The ice was broken.

"Tell us about yourselves, boys," Steve said. "We've got a long way to go."

CHAPTER 20

Wes

It actually took Wes several days to unspool his life story, with long breaks and then sections erupting in bursts of desperate intensity when we had a stretch of time to talk. He seemed worried that any gap in our understanding would leave us, the world watching the events at the refuge, and maybe God—though he denied that part—to judge him. But so much of what happened over the next days and weeks depended on the slightly humorous, slightly tragic set of circumstances that had formed him that it seems worth presenting them now.

He was born in 1984, in Manti, which is a more or less typical-seeming rural Utah town. It's arranged, in the Mormon way, neatly and compactly on a grid at the center of Sanpete Valley—the legacy of Mormon communalism being that unlike in farm towns in the rest of the country, rural Utahans tend to live in tight little neighborhoods and drive out to their alfalfa fields and cow barns to do the day's work. One small irony of this setup is that many small Utah towns, structured in the years of the open range to have tiny home plots surrounded by huge expanses of unclaimed grazing land, are encircled by huge contiguous swathes of federal land, coming right up to the edge of backyards and mostly unbroken by the kind of big private cattle ranches that you find in Wyoming. Ranchers who might be living like aristocrats today if their ancestors had cobbled together a spread of private ground find themselves going to the BLM and the Forest Service and more or less begging for AUMs, and their poorer brethren don't even bother.

The stream-cut valley sits between two high ridges of red and tan shale and sandstone, shrouded in sagebrush and juniper. This is managed by the USFS and is where Wes's family used to run their cattle, before they had to cut back the herd and eventually give it up entirely. Now they stick to a small plot of alfalfa in a rented field just outside town.

His ancestors were Danes who had converted in the mid-1800s, and it was Danish stonemasons who had crossed the desert and built the huge Manti Utah Temple, the biggest for many miles around. It quite literally gleams, in white stone, sitting atop a tall hill at the center of town, and next to it there's a preserved dirt hut, with patchy grass growing over the top of it and a tiny, low door. It looks barely fit to serve as a badger's den, and the point is to remind people that their ancestors were willing to live in houses like that just for the sake of being together in Zion—and that people who lived in such houses built the beautiful stone temple. "Can you fucking imagine?" he said to me once. "These are middle-class people, with trades and houses and everything, and they give all that up and come to Utah, which they have no idea of—there's Indians and mountain lions and everything—and live in a sod hut. It's amazing, right?"

His parents were very religious and very involved in the

community, and he lived a life of sports and Sunday school, shooting guns and driving four-wheelers and getting into trouble when he had a chance. He wrestled and played football, both of which activities came with strict everyday curfews, and he was in the local seminary, training like most Mormon boys to enter the baroque hierarchy of the Church priesthood. But high school wrestling is a religion in that part of the world too. "Back in the day the older guys would grab me and see what I was made of," he told me. "And they were like, you're going to be really good in college. One of the best."

He got a girlfriend, and his wrestling exploits began to appear in the papers in Salt Lake City. "But when I wrestled my knee would come out of place," he said. "And I'd have to like grab it and pop it back in." He toughed through this all the way to the state championship match. "So for the state championship my knee popped out and I just fell facedown on the mat and was lying there and he got those points." A medic came out and got his knee into place. "And then I got up," he said, "and beat his ass."

After graduation he didn't want to leave his girlfriend, and he didn't want to leave Utah, which for him back then probably would have been like a Californian leaving to go to college in Russia. "And they had just cut the wrestling program at UVU," he said. So he stayed in Manti, where his girlfriend was his world. She had had a wild past. He was an almost absurdly righteous young man and a state wrestling champ and popular in school and was getting ready to go on his mission. There's a sort of country-song air of doom in how he talks about the relationship.

She had been out on the fringe of Utah teen culture and been through some dark times, and some of the more moralistic locals reproved her for it. "And so she felt so worthless," he said, "that she'd go out to Spanish Fork.

"Spanish Fork was a big drug town. All the people in Salt Lake and whatnot would jump in their trucks and go down and cruise Main Street," he said. I liked these little pictures of rural Utah youth culture and asked him endless questions on the subject. "Friday and Saturday night there would be a thousand kids down there, buying drugs, doing drugs. And they'd get away with it because they said they were just cruising Main, like it was the sixties with Chevys and shit. But they had diesel trucks, lifted trucks. And she'd just jump in the trucks."

This was all when she was very young. She came back to the Church, and Wes met her when she was a sophomore. "And we loved each other, you know?" he said. "And we wanted to get married. But I also had this overwhelming desire, which is what I was taught I had to do, which is go on a mission. And so I said I had to go on a mission, no matter what.

"And so this girl was just devastated," he told me, "because after she had come out of being crazy and whatnot, I was like her whole life. Because I didn't judge her."

They started fooling around. "I had never had sex before," he said. "I would just ask about it, because I didn't have that experience myself. But when you're a virgin, you don't understand! Especially when you're a Mormon virgin."

We spent hours talking about sex and romance in rural Utah, mostly because I found it fascinating. "Lots of guys are like, how can you marry a girl who has already had sex?" he said. "She'll always want to be having sex with other guys and stuff. I think that's crazy.

"So we ended up having sex two times," he went on. It was right before his graduation from seminary. "In Utah the seminary is right there on the campus and everything," he said. "And I had sex the *weekend before* my seminary graduation.

"And she goes and tells the bishop," he said, "because she felt so bad, which is what you're supposed to do, which is really creepy and weird, right?" The bishop had her disfellowshipped, or put under Church discipline, and he barred Wes from saying the prayer at the seminary graduation—which for his family would have been something like a valedictorian barred from speaking at a high school graduation because he'd been caught plagiarizing a paper, but obviously much worse and much harder to take because the whole thing was laced through with the public airing of sex and shame in a tiny community where no secret or private shame is ever really private or secret. "And it was fucking embarrassing, because my family is *way* conservative, especially my mother," he said. "She's really concerned with what people think."

But he still burned to go on his mission. It's almost impossible to overstate the pressure some Mormon families place on boys to go on a mission—it's like armed service for a Spartan, a universalizing experience that if you skip marks you as somehow not fully a member of the fold. "And so then you have to wait six months to go on your mission after you've had sex. Because they think you're going to want more sex.

"So they basically broke us up," he said. "And I moved to

Salt Lake with my sister. I was miserable—I was *so miserable*, dude. I was doing rain gutters, and my sister knew I needed to get away from my parents, because we were just going at it tooth and nail."

He kept sneaking back to Manti from Salt Lake, a journey of a couple of hours in good traffic, to see her. "And she was hot, dude. I mean, when you're eighteen and full of testosterone? And we dated for three years before we had sex. I mean good Lord." They kept fooling around, and every time that happened his mission got delayed another six months, and he lived on, pulled between an irreconcilable pair of devotions, to her and the Church.

"And finally," he said, "she was like, you either need to move back from Salt Lake or we're breaking up. And I was like, I can't move back, because I have to go on the mission. So we broke up."

Retelling this, he seemed stunned anew by the sadness of it. "And I was fuckin' miserable, dude, I was so fucking miserable. I was destroyed," he said. "I'd go to the college in Manti and see her there and I was just heartbroke. Just heartbroke. And I got ready to go on my mission."

It turned out that Wes, with his wrestling background, had also become a bit of a rising star in the Utah mixed martial arts scene of Brazilian jiu jitsu and submission grappling—both being sort of vaguely like what college wrestling would be if in wrestling you could fight from your back and were allowed to choke your opponent into acquiescence. By coincidence, it turns out that when I'm off the pills and cigarettes I'm a not totally incompetent grappler and fighter, and so we passed a nerdy hour talking about our favorite fighters and tournaments. We made plans to go at it sometime, but I'm sure that with his wrestling background he'd pancake me. "I was so angry all the time, dude," he said. "It was a rough period. I would go do jiu jitsu and just tear people apart, pick them up and slam them on the mat. I barely even knew any submissions, but I was just a monster. They'd have the whole class, like forty guys, try to take me down, and no one could do it. For like hours. And I was just pounding weights like, *I can't have sex I can't have sex I can't get in a fight I can't get in a fight*. Just repeat that to myself."

He went to Argentina for his mission. He learned Spanish, and for two years he moved around the country, living in slums and farms far off in the pampas. His stories about the time are slightly surreal, being the stories of a gringo inhabiting spaces gringos, even the grittiest of authenticity-loving tourists, don't go. "The wild pigs down there," he told me once, "I mean they would kill you. And people see them coming and like scream and run from them. And so one time this hog comes up to the farm and we think it's about to kill this kid so I'm getting ready to, you know, like die and jump on it and see what happens. And all of a sudden this old guy comes out and fricking like nearly turns a knife on me and is yelling and everything and mud is everywhere and it turns out the pig is his guard dog. It was weird out there, man.

"So I got back from my mission," he went on. "But I didn't have any friends, and I was kinda older because I'd had to wait for my mission because I got in trouble." He drove back to Manti every weekend. "I'm a little small-town boy," he said.

"I didn't understand how Salt Lake worked. And in my town they have this little Mormon school called Snow College, and that's where the action was. You know, riding four-wheelers, riding snowmobiles, having bonfires, going out to the hot pots." Hot potting is western party-speak for getting a bunch of kids together and going to bathe in country hot springs. "When you're that age, my community is really fun." He met a new girl.

"She's this little young hottie southern belle from East Texas," he said. "It'd take her like an hour and a half to do her makeup every day." They fell in love. He proposed. "And I was trying to hold off, you know, like, *we're gonna get married*." They waited. "But we ended up fooling around," he said, "and they said we couldn't get married in the Temple."

And so for a second time—the second of the only two big romances he'd ever had—the Church stepped in and derailed his life. Once, Mormons had weddings more or less like anyone else, at a local ward house or with their family, after which they'd go to one of the big temples like the one in Manti, where the most ceremonial acts of the faith are conducted, and they'd be formally sealed to each other for celestial eternity. Mormons also used to drink beer, for that matter. But they were barred from marrying in the temple, and it became the second big mess of shame and public scandal and personal loss in his young adulthood, and it seems to have nearly broken him. "It didn't used to be this big deal of getting married in the temple," Jon Pratt said at one point in this story. "But this society has just got more and more jacked up."

"It's hypocrites and Pharisees," Wes said. Jon himself married his wife in the Manti Utah Temple. "In the Emerald Room," he told us.

"The nicest one," Wes said, sadly. "We already had all our shit paid for," he said. "Tickets for the honeymoon, you know, everything.

"And if you haven't been to Manti you can't understand it," he said. "Like imagine the Salt Lake City temple, but on top of a huge hill in a tiny town. You're literally going to school in the shadow of the temple that your ancestors built, and it's the be-all-end-all of everything. And if you don't get married in that temple, it's a big embarrassment."

I found it baffling how attached he still was then to the rules of the Church, but he said it was the only thing he'd ever known. "I was hard-core about living by the rules," he said. "And she wanted to lie about it, because she knew all the shit-show that was gonna come. And looking back, I probably should have," he said. "Because who gives a shit?

"They make girls feel bad about sex," he said. "For the longest time every girl I had sex with would just start crying—this is Utah."

He got interrogated. "Like, 'How many times did you have sex?'" he said they asked, "'What did you do?' wanting to know specific dates and times. Almost like they're getting off on it.

"Because she was this hot little thing and they were these creepy old dudes," he said. "And her dad hauled her back to Texas. They were trying to say I was like a porn addict, and to blame it all on me, and they did this whole fucking ten-step thing where this guy was like, 'You can become a child molester.'

"And we could have just got married not in the temple," he went on. "But then she was so stressed out and it ruined her life—because everything in her life had built up to that, and you're thinking about your eternal families in the celestial kingdom and all that. Like in Mormonism you don't just go to heaven—there are levels. And you are always trying to get to different positions in the levels, you know? So they hauled her back to Texas.

"And they do this to you, where they're like just pounding you," he said. "And if you ever look at anything on TV with boobs or whatever, they're like, 'Oh you looked at porn.' And it's like, 'No! That's fricking on TV!' "

This time he really began to break with the Church. "I was like, 'Okay, I can't do this anymore,' " he said. "I'm broken." He had, at twenty-five, his first drink, at a party with some kids from Nebraska. "I had a couple shots of Jack Daniel's straight out of the freezer, which was fucking amazing," he said. "I got a sore throat for like a week after that, 'cause I had never really drank. But I fooled around with a girl with these big ole boobs that night, so I was like, 'Drinking is awesome!' You know?

"Then I just partied it up, dude," he said. "All summer 2009, going to bonfires, going to sand dunes. I was carrying a fucking blender around, dude. I had a good ole fucking time."

He started hanging out with people he called "party people," having fun, and getting drunk, and talking to the crowd he'd been brought up to avoid and that somehow had still spent most of his adulthood avoiding.

"And I was like, 'This is fucking awesome!' People are happy, they're having a good time," he said. "They aren't always judging each other all the time. And it was right after I had wanted to kill myself."

So he left Utah and went up to North Dakota to work on oil rigs. Company men liked him because he was tough. He won fights, worked hard, and made a lot of money. And he began to lose his faith. "I'd have my mind opening," he said. "I kept coming back and I'd have girlfriends and they'd make us break up, because I wouldn't go to church.

"And then one day I had pneumonia," he said. "They gave me codeine syrup. And I remember being just so fucking high, even though I was on the normal dose, and all of a sudden I was open to like liberal thoughts, and philosophy and stuff. Because I remember going through college and listening to things like that and doing the Mormon thing of hardening your heart, and holding to your testimony—this constant drumbeat of 'I-know-the-church-is-true, I-know-Joseph-Smith-is-a-prophet.'" He beat his hands together to punctuate every word.

"So it's been a progression," he said, "like I still have staunch views like on gun rights and land use and stuff." He thought for a minute. "But I also feel really bad for refugees—like imagine being a child or someone who's been through war, and you come to a country where people hate you and are discriminating against you?"

He seemed, in a way that I identified with completely, to have come to a sort of typical millennial juncture. He had enough money to almost seem surprised at it, such that he could buy trucks and guns and go out and party loud when he wanted, but it was never going to be near enough to bring his family back to ranching or any kind of life that he'd been brought up to recognize as a desirable adulthood. He'd been unmoored from the social strictures and religion that defined his parents' life, and he was casting about for meaning and a cause, which in the absence of his childhood religion probably had as much to do with some pretty fair existential questions of why he ought to wake up every morning and what he ought to do all day as it did with any true hatred of the federal government. "I used to Bible-battle people and fucking destroy them, dude. I knew thirty to forty pages of scripture by heart. I was obsessed." Now he had thought going off to join the YPG to fight ISIS, which would have made for a funny alternate future for his story, because the foreigners who have joined the YPG have mostly been westerners with dreams of building a left-wing revolution in Syria. But his abiding concern was with the same thing preoccupying the townspeople at the meeting in Burns, a desperate and totally genuine love for an idea of a communally minded and free-living western way of life that corporate agriculture and federal regulations were supposedly squeezing out of existence. I don't think you have to idealize this sort of thing, support the Bundys, or believe in a glossy magical cowboy past to take this kind of love seriously. And not that I think it absolves him of what happened in Oregon, and not to forgive any of the people he ended up casting his lot with for their ludicrous obsession with fake environmental conspiracies capturing the federal government, or their racist hysteria about Sharia law being somehow enacted in the Great Basin and usurping their culture. But it was this feeling that Wes was responding to when Ammon took over the refuge.

"So I quit my job," he said. "I had three days left on a two-week hitch, and there was a bunch of drama on that rig anyway. I said I was curious about it, interested in being maybe a supporter. And they were like, 'So, will you take a bullet?'"

CHAPTER 21

The Prophet and the Acolyte

It's possible we didn't pass a single car between Burns and the Idaho line. The snow kept up for the first hour or so as we climbed toward the pass and then cleared as we headed into the flat expanse of potato fields. Wes talked about Argentina and Jon lay in the back while Steve and Todd gave a sort of comedy-routine initiation into Mormon life and their years in the Liberty Movement, traveling around the West for conferences and working on writings about the Constitution. Steve talked in manic floods, frequently letting go of the steering wheel to wave his hands. Todd sat very still, pursing his mustache and talking so slowly and officiously that Steve would get amped up again and cut him off mid-sentence. "Now Steve," he kept saying.

"You aren't letting me talk!" Steve said. "I'm your friend and you should let me talk." There was a bit of small-town psychodrama going on. "Or at least I hope I can call you my friend."

"You're my friend, Steve," Todd said deliberately, like a judge sustaining an objection.

"I'm very glad to hear that," Steve said. He turned to us. "We'd never had that conversation officially."

Steve had been infuriated by the PPN parading around like an occupying army, and his point in talking about Mormonism to me was to say that no one could understand what was happening at the refuge without understanding the Mormon tendency to fall behind prophets. "The prophet-and-follower is built into the whole religion, into the whole community," he said.

"I'd say that's true," Todd affirmed.

"It's very true!" Steve said. "And Ammon has set himself up as a prophet!" He was getting more and more worked up as we approached Idaho. He was talking in torrents now, and we lost the road and found ourselves on a gravel track hugging the state line, doing twenty miles an hour. This was halfway my fault—I'd been assigned to navigate, but I was so thrown by the intensity of the conversation that I forgot to look at my phone. "And LaVoy is following him as a prophet because it's what we've all been taught!"

At the time, none of us knew how right Steve was. More than a year later, while we sat chatting at the Texas Station casino, I asked Shawna Cox about why Ammon had been so driven to take over the refuge. She said casually he'd told her that an angel had visited him three times one night and told him he had to help the Hammonds. It didn't matter that the Hammonds themselves had declaimed the whole standoff— Ammon was acting on higher orders.

"But at the same time, Ammon is resisting tyranny," Wes

said. "Like, how did they know the American Revolution was justified?" I think, though we've never talked about it, that Wes and I both were being forced to think uncomfortable new thoughts about the reality and consequences of political violence, to think about what would happen to the parents and kids of people at the refuge if they ended up dead or in prison. Which of course would have forced Wes to think about how gutted his own parents would be.

"This isn't tyranny in that sense," Steve said, and launched into an Ammonesque disquisition on natural rights and definitions of tyranny that got him so worked up that he pulled the car over so he could wave his hands in earnest. It was both moving and totally ridiculous. Wes looked dazed. Jon and I somehow suddenly found the situation hilarious, us in a weird limousine truck pulled halfway into a ditch somewhere near Pocatello so Steve could convince this stranger—who incidentally was quite possibly being pursued by federal authorities—that he'd been conned by a false prophet. We started laughing, which annoyed Steve, which made us laugh more, until we were laughing so hard our stomachs hurt and it began to feel like cruel mockery, but we were too gone to stop.

"This is important!" Steve was screaming. "How is this funny! This is the lives of people!"

Todd finally intervened. "Now Steve," he said. "We're all taking you seriously," which really was true. "It's just that we're in a ditch." We pulled back onto the road.

"So if Ammon has set himself up as a prophet . . ." Wes said. He seemed particularly disturbed to think that he'd fallen into a Mormon thought pattern, one that these guys had been wise enough to resist. "Then . . ." He really seemed shaken. "And he's not listening to anyone because he thinks he's talking to God, then anything could happen to those people . . ."

"This is my thing with them," Todd said. He'd known various members of the family for years. "They don't listen to anyone. And that's why I've never drunk the Bundy Kool-Aid."

"Oh, man, Ammon just texted me," Wes said. He was going rapidly from bothered to despondent. "Miss you already," it read. "Hope you're safe." He let that hang there for a minute. "You know the thing is, he does trust me," he said.

The Church had already issued a public statement condemning the occupation, and talk turned to whether or not Ammon would end up being excommunicated. I asked if he'd care. "Yeah, you don't know what that would do to him," Steve said to me.

"It would be very hard," Todd said. "He doesn't want that."

Wes told a story about a phone call he'd overheard, when someone speaking for the First Presidency, a three-person directorship headed by a titular prophet that formed the temporal leadership of the Church, had supposedly reached out to Ammon and asked him to stand down.

"That's interesting," Jon said. He'd sat up by now and taken off his hat. "I wonder how he responded to that."

"I bet he didn't listen," Steve said. We crossed into Utah. "I hope you boys don't need any booze," he said. "We're under the Zion Curtain." It was around two in the morning, and we were all very awake. It was about to be Sunday morning. "You really can't understand any of this if you don't understand Mormonism," Steve said, and suddenly he got taken with an idea. "You want to go to church?" he asked me. I said that I'd be happy to.

Steve had been pulling back from the Church, and it had apparently been a bit of a domestic issue. "I can't wait to see the look on your wife's face if she saw you show up in church with these guys in tow," Todd said.

"She might not survive the shock," Steve said. We headed down I-15 toward Salt Lake.

"So are you married?" Todd asked me. I said I wasn't. "And do you have a girlfriend? Or, I mean, another kind of . . . ?" It occurred to me for the first time that I presented an even more exotic figure to them than they did to me, and it felt nice to have someone take enough of an interest to ask questions. I said that I'd been breaking up and not breaking up with a girl for years. They asked why we hadn't married, and I said that it was hard to say exactly, but that every day for the past few months I'd regretted that I'd been brought up into a culture so obsessed with youth and choice and freedom that when I was younger I'd felt—almost like Wes feeling like he had to go on his mission—that I had no choice but to drink up experience for experience's sake, to sleep with new partners in numbers that had gone far past my ability to count or account for in terms of human connection, and that I increasingly felt confused as to why it had once been so important to me that I get away from Cincinnati, why I'd spent a decade consumed with physical displacement and bedding women and how it had only just in recent months become clear to me how much every week I spent away from my family felt empty and directionless. I said that in a way they were making Mormonism sound kind of nice.

"It's like the opposite of the Mormon issue," Steve said. "Mission, marriage, church, work." I said I was faintly jealous. Todd asked if I was religious. I said that I'd been raised Quaker, sitting through silent meetings and going to potlucks and pretending to be a pacifist, but hadn't been able to get into it. Then one day, living in New Orleans and having my relationship with the girl implode, I'd suddenly started to see divinity everywhere. We both moved to Los Angeles, separately, and became sort of enchanted with how inescapably intertwined our fates had seemed to be. We started going to Mass together and were surprised at how much we liked it. I told them about how when we stopped talking I fell into my obsession with growing and propagating sagebrushes, which I think they found endearing if only because these were the plants that had colored the standoff and the whole lives of all these men. I had developed a bit of a chip on my shoulder, because the nice ladies and occasionally not-nice bearded young men at the various native-plant nurseries I went to were always telling me I was doing things wrong or that some particular plant couldn't survive in some particular spot where I'd put it. The truth was that I'd had no real idea what I was doing, but I found that I *got* the plants, in a way that I had a lot of trouble fully describing, and that I could make them do whatever I wanted. They were my buddies. I knew what they needed and how to ask for stuff from them. Again, I was very lonely. But I had trouble understanding my garden—and in fact the ways in which the genus *Artemisia* became so oddly entwined with my life—as something other than a religious experience, and I saw no real reason to push back from the feeling. And that a more searching spirituality had started to flow from there.

There was a pause. I regretted talking. "I understand that," Todd said. "I don't think it's that different for any of us. Especially in regard to the land." Light was edging into the horizon, and we could see junipers appearing on the snowy hills beyond the highway. I love junipers, as common and weedy as they are in the West, and I identify with them because I think they're scrappy little fuckers. I made a guess, given that they were just appearing, at what our elevation must have been. I was pretty close.

Todd laughed. "That's not bad," he said. "You might actually know more than we'd give an urban cowboy credit for."

We drove on. Everyone was a bit frayed, having not slept, but we mostly seemed to be in good spirits. The exception was Wes, who by now was shaken by the thought that people were going to die and that he was enabling it and that he'd been brought into a web of spiritual persuasion by Ammon. "I'm just wondering," he said, as we approached Salt Lake City. "What would happen if we went to the First Presidency and asked them, like, with me being a person who Ammon knows and trusts, to pass a message saying . . . I don't know, just a personal message to try to get through to him. Like if he won't listen to anyone else, he might listen to them."

I considered this idea so insane at first that I barely paid any attention to it. Jon sat up. "It's not impossible," he said.

"And if we could save lives," Wes said. "I mean, they're going to know who we are."

We were talking about the Mormon equivalent of showing up at Vatican Square on Sunday morning and asking for an audience with the pope. I was baffled.

"I don't think it's crazy," Steve said. Todd concurred. Jon concurred. "They are watching this whole thing very closely," Jon said.

"Well, it's your call," Steve said. "We can take you to the airport and get you a rental car, and you and James can go get your stuff and go back to the refuge. Or we can go to Temple Square, and then who knows what happens, but you're trying something and I think we'll all respect that."

"Let's go to Temple Square," Wes said.

CHAPTER 22

At the Foot of the Temple I

We parked the rig off the square, the light of morning coming up over the Wasatch Range and illuminating the huge white bulk of the temple itself. We decided that it would be Wes, Jon, and I who actually made the approach, but we all got out and walked to the square. Blond girls in their Sunday best and stony security men in gray suits were moving purposefully around, getting ready for the church rush. It was cold and quiet.

We huddled for a group prayer, and by coincidence we found ourselves next to a set of carved granite tablets quoting from Mormon scripture and outlining the principles of the faith. "Oh, man," Wes said, pointing to one. "Read this." We all gathered.

"The laws and constitution of the people," it began. It was a quote from Doctrine and Covenants, the second book revealed to Joseph Smith, ". . . should be maintained for the rights and protection of all flesh according to just and holy principles; that every man may act according to the moral agency given unto him, that every man may be accountable for his own sins in the day of judgment."

"How is that a coincidence? That we stand by that?" Wes said.

"It's not," Steve said.

Wes denied this later, but it was hard not to think that some inner faith had been reactivated in him. He seemed filled with wonder and with a huge amount of trepidation at the spiritual and temporal power of this church, into whose hands he was giving himself over again. He led the prayer, and his voice cracked on the words "Dear Lord," tears running down his face by the end.

Then Todd and Steve went back to the truck, and Jon approached a security guard.

Jon's great-great-great-grandfather Parley Pratt had been the first great apostle of the faith, and you wouldn't have needed to know this or to have shared the Mormon obsession with ancestors to see him channeling something as his posture straightened.

We must have made a strange sight, three grimy men in cowboy boots, looking around for a security man at dawn on a Sunday morning. Jon located one, an older guy with a flat-top haircut and a gray suit who looked very much like he was still living in the '50s. In the way he carried himself and gave orders, it would come to seem like he wasn't a simple security guard either, but what kind of role in the baroque hierarchy of the Church he might have played was something none of us could figure out.

"We came here from the Bundy standoff," Jon said simply.

"I can believe that," the security man said, examining us quickly. Jon looked impressive—tall and lean and speaking slowly, firmly, and like what was happening was the most normal thing in the world. He told him about Wes, and said we'd like to communicate with the First Presidency. The man had been manipulating his radio earpiece while this was happening, and we were quickly surrounded by more stern, thick men in gray suits. The head man said it was impossible and strongly suggested that we get out of there.

"Do you know the name Pratt?" Jon asked. The man nodded. "Well, my name is Jon Pratt," he said. I found it amazing how much an effect this seemed to have on the security men. "I know this is something the Church cares a great deal about. And you're going to get us someone to talk to." They were powerless.

Wes was sitting there shivering, looking at his feet. "Do you have any weapons on you?" the man asked. Wes felt around. "I have this pocketknife I forgot about," he said, taking it out. "I'm really sorry."

"I'm not worried about a pocketknife, son," he said. A spoken word service and performance of the Mormon Tabernacle Choir was about to start, and, surreally, they asked if we wanted to sit in. We still hadn't eaten or slept, but Steve and Todd rejoined us and we went. The sermon was arranged as a teaching on the danger of charismatic leaders. Wes cried through a lot of it. "I was just thinking about how people I knew could get killed," he said. "And it's a charismatic leader! And they're talking about it here. I don't know, man."

The security men surrounded us again. "We have a meeting set up," he said. "But it's going to be a minute." We stood around. One of the guards, a younger guy with a buzz cut, seemed starstruck by all of us. "They're doing good work up there in Oregon," he said. Jon let him talk. "You know we've got a lot of problems down here in Utah," he went on. He began to mention names of people in the PPN and the Oath Keepers and asked if we knew them. "I really respect those guys," he said. He asked what Ammon was like. The man with the flat-top haircut began to use body language to advertise his displeasure. The younger guy shut up. "The Church can't control this stuff," Steve told me later. "All they can do is control their image."

I interjected and said that if I didn't have a cup of coffee I might have a meltdown, and then suddenly caught myself thinking maybe this wouldn't be the best look to be putting on in front of a Mormon security man. "Or just, I mean, I can live without it," I said. He winked at me. "Get yourself some coffee, son," he said.

We loaded up the rig and drove to a Denny's. We were openly tailed, and it seemed like someone from the church must have called the FBI. I found it horribly stressful, watching the hatchback Nissan tailing us through the city; watching the guy who sat down to watch us in our booth as he talked on the phone for an hour and took only two bites of a full stack of chocolate chip pancakes. Steve had gone into full-on paranoiac mode and was busily picking arguments with random people he thought were FBI agents.

"Keep looking," he yelled over to a table where a young stoner-hippie-looking couple was sitting waiting for eggs.

"Uh," the guy said.

"We're right here," Steve said. "You don't have to hide it."

"Dude, I don't know you," the stoner guy said.

"Mhm," Steve said. "Yeah, you don't."

"We're going to get arrested just for making a scene," Jon said.

"Who cares at this point?" Wes said.

"They aren't fooling me," Steve said.

The confusing thing was that we were definitely being watched but that we weren't sure by whom, and somehow in our fatigue and pretty fair worry that Wes—or, hell, all of us—might be about to get taken down, we'd lost the sense of what was a normal level of concern and what was adrenaline-fueled paranoia. Soon we got a text from the church saying that our meeting was set, and we loaded up the rig, the little white Nissan dutifully trailing behind again. It would have been funny to see, if anyone could have known what was going on—a giant limousine truck trundling around downtown Salt Lake halfheartedly trying to shake a tail even though we couldn't have picked a more conspicuous vehicle if we'd tried, while the tiny hatchback followed behind, the driver not bothering at all to try to conceal that he was tailing us. We headed back to the church, where we were rushed up to the second floor of the Joseph Smith Memorial Building. Steve stayed with the truck, driving around Salt Lake and pausing occasionally to send disturbing pictures of white vans assembled outside. Inside it was quiet and ornate in a vaguely Trump Tower sort of way, full of polished brass, rich woods, thick carpets, and lush wallpaper. I called my editor, who had once been the first call I'd made after getting put in jail due to trainhopping-related issues, and arranged with him to call my family and to request info on my whereabouts from the FBI if he didn't hear from me by the afternoon. Then I went and joined the meeting with the Church officials.

We'd all agreed that quotes from the meeting and the names of the participants, though not the gist of what we talked about and the circumstances surrounding it, would be off the record. Part of this was because the men from the church seemed very concerned that Wes might be in danger from Patriot groups if word of it got out. They were even more concerned that the Church be kept as far away from the whole thing as possible, and they came off as unbearably slimy, working hard to seem interested without actually implicating the Church at all. Wes seemed totally despondent, exhausted, and humiliated at having put himself in the power of men like them. Jon and Todd were unrelenting, and basically made it clear that they wouldn't leave until the Church agreed to take some sort of concrete action to reach out to Ammon directly. Finally they said that they'd go to Ammon's stake president—a role sort of like that of a bishop in a small Catholic diocese—and have him place a call relaying that he was still welcome in the fold and making a personal appeal to him, on behalf of the Church, to stand down.

Steve was still texting me as he drove around waiting for us to finish. I showed everyone the lineup of white vans he'd sent me, and we worked up a plan in which I'd go out first to smoke a much-needed cigarette while I waited for Steve to pull up outside of the building and Wes, Todd, and Jon waited for me to throw them a signal to hurry Wes out into the car. This came off unbelievably smoothly, with all of us hoisting ourselves into the rig almost before it had stopped moving. By this time Steve seemed to have lost touch with reality and was taunting by text an FBI agent he knew and imagining tails coming from every car we passed. Jon took over driving. But all of us had crossed somewhere into a paranoid alternate reality where it seemed like the arrest would come at any minute. Our nerves were so frayed that if we didn't get somewhere and retrench soon one of us might crack up. Jon and Todd conferred for a while, and eventually we decided to head down to their home in Kanosh, where their wives could feed us and we could get a motel room anonymously and sleep some before Wes and I had to go back up to the refuge and get his Jeep and his guns, because he was done with what was happening up there.

CHAPTER 23

Lying There in the Dark

We drove on to Todd's house and had the most welcome dinner I'd ever eaten, served by his incredibly friendly and easygoing wife, Heidi. We ate turkey cutlets and potatoes and greens and there was raw goat milk from their farm and fresh-baked cookies. Todd and Jon set us up with a fellow named Bob, who ran the local gas station and an attached motel, which happened to be the only place in town where we could buy beer. He was gnarled and sweet.

"Six-pack?" I asked.

"We need a case," Wes told him.

"My man," I said.

We were the only people at the motel. I went out to smoke a cigarette and call my ex-girlfriend. She'd moved in with a new guy, and a few weeks before, when my uncle had just died and I tried to crash her family Christmas, which happened to have been on my driving route from New York back home to Cincinnati, she wouldn't take my calls. But this time she picked up and listened while I told a slightly frantic version of the events of the past few days. While we were talking I stepped out from the doorway and startled a youngish bearded man idling a late-model white Ford SUV a block south of the motel. He put it into gear, slowly pulled into the closed gas station, and pantomimed the act of refueling. He wore slim cargo pants and looked like someone I might have once run into in a bar in Brooklyn. It seemed very implausible that he lived in Kanosh, Utah. We matched looks from about fifty yards away, as he held the pump. I made a sort of shrug with one shoulder and he did it back and then got in the car and drove off. I stamped out my cigarette, went back inside, and then changed my mind and decided I wanted another. I was still on the phone. The guy turned out onto the main drag south of us again—he must have driven north and looped around on back streets. This time he drove past without acknowledging me and parked about half a mile north of the motel. He stayed for the next couple of hours, until just before bed I came out for a last cigarette and he was gone.

Wes and I were buds by now. We watched westerns on the TV and talked about jiu jitsu and MMA. Wes seemed adamant that I not think he was a terrorist. "I'm a moderate!" he kept saying. "I mean, I guess I like some of the stuff Trump is saying, like about extremism." Both our heads cocked, and we started laughing at the same time. "Yeah, I guess it's kind of weird for *me* to be talking about extremism." He asked what I thought he should do, and I said that I thought he ought to go up and get his stuff, have a conversation with Ammon, and then go straight home. I think he was worried about being taken for an informer or a coward, and he was still, amazingly, worried about jeopardizing his relationship with Ammon. I asked why he even cared. "You just get close to someone when you're lying there in the dark with drones and stuff flying around," he said. "Does that make sense?" I said it did, and that I felt like in the last day I'd got a more intimate sense of his character, and those of Todd, Jon, and Steve, than I had of a lot of my friends.

We talked about girls. "I've got this girl I'm talking to in Salt Lake," he said. "And she's texting me like, what's up? But what am I supposed to tell her now, like—did you see that thing on TV? With the crazy like guerrilla army? That's me!" We fell asleep. I woke us both up in the middle of the night, when I had a dream I got chased by cops off the roof of a building. I sat up waving my arms and shouting at the top of my voice. "That was, uh, really fucking loud, dude," Wes said. He was understating it. I'd been shouting so loud my chest hurt, and I was gasping to get my breath back. "You okay?" I was mortified. He was very sweet about it. "You just had a frightmare is all," he said. I said I'd never had a dream like that, and we went back to sleep.

We ate breakfast at Todd and Heidi's. Jon and his wife, Jessie—a slightly ethereal brunette who has since made me wonderful meals and seems oddly like she would fit very well teaching yoga or doing art in Brooklyn, except that she also homeschools six kids and is as tough and competent out of doors as I'll probably ever be—drove up from their house south of town. I like to visit down there with them, and it's a country wonderland in the middle of nowhere, where Jon and various members of the family customize trucks and run a forge and a gunsmithy and fabricate old wagons and artifacts for reenactments and historical displays. There are usually uncountable children and dogs running around, and all in all it's a very fun place to be. "I was at this meeting with these polygamists a while ago," he told me. "And they were saying that any time a polygamist puts a fence around a property it's a 'compound,' but that when other people do the same thing it's an 'estate,' and they'd like people to use that term. So I figure that then we get to call this the 'Pratt Estate.'"

We decided that we'd all drive up to Provo, which was two hours away but the closest place we could rent a car, and then Wes and I would drive back to the refuge. It seemed obvious enough, based on the man outside the motel the night before, that someone knew where we were—old man Bob certainly hadn't phoned us in and probably hadn't even taken down our names, and it didn't seem that we'd been followed all the way from Salt Lake. But in any case we all figured, wrongly, as it turned out, that if they were going to come for Wes they would have already done it, and that on those grounds he'd be safe renting a car. I still felt like it'd be crossing a line to have the car in my name, though when the time came I let them put me down as an added driver, if only for expediency's sake. I was still very worried about crossing any sort of line that would have had me helping Ammon and what was happening up at the refuge, but now it felt like I'd just be helping Wes to get away, and anyway, I've always hated to be a passenger in a car I might otherwise be driving.

We set off for Provo. Wes was worried about what he was going to say to Ammon, and I think, though he didn't want to put it this way, he was worried that if Ammon asked him to stay he wouldn't be able to leave. He was quiet, while we all joked and laughed about how spooked we'd been by the real and imagined tails through Salt Lake and I babbled about plants I liked to grow.

"Jon," Wes said suddenly. "I was wondering if you could come back with us, if you could talk to Ammon with me." The car was very quiet. Jon didn't have any stuff with him, he had a sick child at home, and he'd already been away from work back at the Pratt Estate long enough that he almost hadn't been able to spare the two hours to come with us to Provo. But it made sense—the man radiated no bullshit without needing to act tough, and, at least for Mormons, there seemed to be some sort of spiritual power residing in his last name. Wes had worked very hard to get away from this sort of throbbing, constant power of Church and history that he'd grown up with, but I think that at this point he was willing to take whatever help he could get.

So Jon agreed, and the three of us loaded into a rented slate-gray Corolla. We stopped at a Sportsman's Warehouse to buy a locking case for Wes's AR in case he got pulled over on his way home, and we headed back up I-15 toward Boise. We were past Salt Lake by early afternoon, and I took the driver's seat near dusk. To our right, the red-and-white wall of the snowy Wasatch Mountains was lit up by the setting sun, and by chance "Mamas, Don't Let Your Babies Grow Up to Be Cowboys" came on the stereo. "That's pretty appropriate, isn't it?" Wes said. We got back to Burns at three in the morning and took a motel room. By seven fifteen we were up and driving the lonely road back to the refuge.

CHAPTER 24

A Hard Conversation to Be Having

We got back to what seemed like a shaggy carnival of misfits. Which was good to see, because, stuck in the office with the spiritual calm of the leaders all day, it was easy to forget that this was how most of the world saw what was happening at the refuge. Sean and Sandy Anderson, the nutty couple from Wisconsin, were at the gate that morning, lecturing a journalist named Hal Herring, from Alabama by way of Montana, about liberty and guns and abortion and things. He listened to them more or less silently until they got to the abortion part. "I know as much about liberty as either of you," he told them, "and if you ever try to tell my daughter what she can or can't do with her body, you'll see real quick how I exercise my gun rights." It turned out that he was a sort of backwoods, book-loving, left-wing gun nut—my favorite kind of person—and loved his AR as much as any of them. Sean literally gulped and went quiet.

There was a legless man sitting on a stump, talking about how he'd found Jesus after losing his legs—he said he'd been a marine officer—and how there in that circle around the fire he felt God's light so intensely that he needed us all to kneel and pray with him, which meant he needed to get down out of his seat. This meant someone had to lift him and set him on his stumps in the snow. Two militia guys tried but lost hold and let him topple over until he fell down almost into the fire, and so then Hal and I had to help lift him back up, and finally he said a long and self-congratulatory prayer about what self-less hero patriots all of us around the fire were, and how clear it must be to all of us that God had directed this takeover and would look after all of us as long as we were faithful to the cause.

I told Hal that if he wanted I could take him back past the gate. "Is it always like this?" he asked. I told him to try to keep away from the crazies hanging around the parking area and the bunkhouse—partly because they were annoying, and partly because most of them didn't have any role in the occu-pation besides eating the food, staying for a couple of days, and babbling psycho right-wing inanities to wandering reporters, who then wrote extremely confused stories about what the whole thing was about. These people had multiplied in our absence.

I introduced him to Duane Ehmer, a goofy metalworker in his midforties, with a big red nose and a high-honking, drawly, country voice, who had become the unlikely icon of the occupation after he showed up with a big old black-powder revolver on his hip and a gelding named Hellboy in a horse trailer behind his old red pickup. He had taken to riding Hell-boy on "patrol" every morning, wearing a cowboy hat and carrying a huge American flag on a staff, as he picked his way through the snow and the sage, the flag fluttering stark against the purple mountains behind him. Photographers couldn't get enough of it. He was soon facing seventeen years in prison.

I left them and went for a smoke. I'd wanted to give Wes some private time with Ammon, but Jon found me and said he thought I should be there, so I left the cigarette—number four of the young day—and went to the office. Inside there was a huckster claiming to be some sort of judge, talking some kind of sovereign citizen nonsense about how he could deputize people at the refuge as marshals. This judge is now in jail in Colorado, facing twenty-four years in prison for issuing fake liens against government officials. We listened for a while, and then suddenly Wes snapped and stood up. "Can I get some private time with Ammon, please?" he said, in a way that did not exactly sound like a question. The fake judge said he'd wait outside, and Ammon and Wes went upstairs.

Wes was very torn up. At first I'd thought of his coming to the refuge as a sort of fluke—a lost boy trundling into an adventure and getting in a bit over his head, and on those grounds it seemed like an obvious step, now that he'd caught his breath a bit, to pack up his stuff and get the hell out of town. But until the drive back I hadn't fully realized how deeply Ammon's worldview already ran in places like where Wes had grown up—how in coming to the refuge Wes hadn't so much discovered a new ideology as he had stepped up for one that had been swirling around him all his life. And if you took the basic premise of that ideology, and of a certain brand of western mythos—that the sanctity of the Constitution and American freedom and a way of life were all things worth dying for, and that real patriots (and real men) were not afraid to die for what they believed in—then by leaving, he was essentially admitting that he didn't believe in it anymore, or that he was a coward and afraid of dying or going to jail.

I know him pretty well now, and I've seen him throw himself on the line over extremely minor slights to his honor or when he thought he'd seen someone wronged—and my honest take is that I don't think he would have left out of fear or worry. Which is to say he had a conversion moment, away from an ideology that to some extent had shaped him all his life, and he was leaving a position that had made him suddenly visible and important and given him the feeling that for the first time in his life he was, as Ammon would have said, *taking a stand*. And in some corners of the world—his corners of the world—that stand was something that could make him look like a real hero. This isn't an exaggeration. A year and a half after the standoff strangers in rural Utah would still find out who he was and treat him like a full-on celebrity for having gone up to Oregon—I know because I saw it happen. But he decided to leave.

"That has got to be a hard conversation to be having," Jon said. After a few minutes they tramped back down. I never learned exactly what was said. They both looked downcast.

"They took over the Verizon wireless store in town," Ryan said, talking about the FBI. "So now they know every stinking thing we say right when we say it." Ammon registered this noncommittally. He seemed genuinely sad and sat, for once, without his big brown cowboy hat, sort of slumped forward in the swivel chair at his desk. He spoke even more gently than he usually did and seemed at pains to justify himself. "You know, we had a choice," he said, to no one in particular. "We could sit with our heads in the sand and live as best we could, and watch destruction come around us. Or we could stand up and deal with it now while we have a chance. And that's what the Lord wanted us to do, and that's what we're doing."

He sounded only half convinced, and his voice trailed off. It was an oddly tender moment, in that Wes's leaving seemed to have really affected him. But it gave us all an ominous feeling. Until then, even when Wes was freaking out and having visions of people dying and getting thrown in jail, I had still somehow thought this would all resolve itself more or less quietly, that Ammon would sense an out at some point in the next few days or even hours, claim a victory, and accept the offer the sheriff had made to peacefully escort them all out of the county. But even in this human moment, the only response he could form was to say that he knew he was doing what God wanted—and by implication that the rest of us, who lacked his clarity of insight into what God wanted, could go off and wait to see the "destruction come around us," if that's what we wanted to do. But either way he, Ammon Bundy, was going to pursue this thing until he won or until he hit a barrier he couldn't smash through. And that, with God on his side, he had trouble conceiving of such a barrier.

I sat with him while Wes and Jon loaded Wes's gear into his Jeep. "So what happened down there?" Ammon said, and I told him the gist of it. "You went to church?" he said, laughing a little. I said I didn't know if the Tabernacle Choir broadcast counted, but that I guessed I had. "What are you going to do now?" he asked. Mostly I wanted to go back to New York and do what I would have been doing if I hadn't come out to Oregon, which was smoking spliffs and watching movies in bed until the winter passed, but we both realized that I was tied up in this thing now, not that he was going to be giving my situation much thought. I said I'd probably stay until the end, and he gave a slight cock of the head, as though to say I was being presumptuous to think there was going to be an end. Wes, Jon, and I caravanned out of the refuge, Jon in front in the rented Corolla and me following behind Wes's Jeep, so we could have half a chance of obscuring his license plates from the cameras the FBI had set up on the telephone poles on the road to the refuge. We had lunch at the not-bad Mexican place on Broadway in Burns and they went off back to Utah.

CHAPTER 25

There's the Flashbang

The FBI was everywhere—on the refuge, in town, on the back roads, in the skies above—and yet was almost always nearly impossible to perceive. Agents had set up a command center at the airport a few miles east of Burns, which put them a good thirty-five miles from the actual gates of the refuge. The distance was deliberate. They had seen how things went bad at the Bundy ranch. The agents who would be involved in any kind of firefight or assault were members of the bureau's Hostage Rescue Team, which had led the disaster of an operation at Waco, and had learned that overt sieges rarely worked out well for anyone. Everyone on the refuge knew that the HRT guys were around, and the more fidgety ones talked about them like they were ghosts, or SS officers, or both—a sort of federal hit squad that you never saw until they kicked in the door, tossed a flashbang, and started firing. This became a sort of dark joke. A guy would drop a glass or slam a door and someone would roll his eyes and say, "There's the flashbang! HRT coming in." It was the sort of thing that was funny because it was plausible.

The Special Agent in Charge of the operation, Greg Bretzing, was rumored to be of a Mormon background, Mormon agents sat alongside the Bundys in church, and it seems fair to assume that with regard to Ammon, Ryan, LaVoy, and Shawna, he believed that he was dealing with people with whom he could have a friendly and seemingly reasonable conversation, but without shaking, at all, their conviction and sense of divine purpose. And nothing he did gives much indication that he bothered to try, which is probably to his credit. He wasn't going to get conned, or dragged into a long negotiation about the fairness of the cause or the right of the government to police this land, and in view of his public statements during the standoff he barely even seemed to have a side in the whole thing. Which, again, was probably deliberate and to his credit. There are several things that FBI agents did at the Bundy ranch, and later up in Oregon, that I find just mendacious and vile— like lying about shots they fired and sending undercover agents to pose as journalists, which is the kind of thing that well could have got someone like me killed. But if anyone found fault with the FBI's handling of the first three weeks of the occupation, it was because its people were too gentle.

Their invisibility at the gates of the refuge was itself a sort of trap. The town of Burns felt like a siege zone. Agents set up unsubtle cameras at intersections around town, and as the days rolled on and the journalists filtered out, they took over room after room at the Days Inn. In the mornings you'd see them loading into big unmarked SUVs, or the techs working out tangles in big spools of wire that they were loading into the back of black vans. I watched as they set up a surveillance camera on a telephone wire right over the motel driveway. Up at the airport they'd assembled a force that probably could have stormed into Canada and occupied Winnipeg if they had a mind to. And they'd established a perimeter of surveillance that let them sit back and wait, letting everyone at the refuge either fall into a complacent lull—as a few did—or boil under the pressure of knowing that the strike could come at any time, and that there'd be no warning.

It was obvious, or at least it should have been, that whatever form the strike took would come in a situation where the FBI had an overwhelming advantage of force and planning, because from the beginning of the occupation to the final moments the whole scene was being relayed back to FBI headquarters by informants.

This is a hard thing to talk about, because it seems misplaced to use a book to expose an informant who hasn't been outed in some more official venue, and because a lot of the informants at the refuge were outed in a set of sealed documents allegedly leaked by a defense attorney to a conspiracy-minded extremist blogger named Gary Hunt, who merrily went on to publish them online before the federal government subpoenaed him to take them down and eventually had him arrested and held until he redacted the documents. I saved all his posts on my hard drive, and since, when I asked, the government declined to dispute the actual accuracy of them, it seems fair at least to draw a few quotes and conclusions.

There seem to have been at least nine informants on the refuge. One of the very first people I talked to when I got there seems to have been an informant, and he was one of the sternest, meanest, most hard-core-seeming militia types I met my whole time there. I know it's a sort of truism to say that the guy you least expect is the one who's most likely to be a snitch, but it still threw me. "No alcohol has been observed and approximately six people have been seen carrying side arms and long guns," read his report for the day I got there. He's referred to in the write-up as CHS, for Confidential Human Source. "CHS has been looking for explosives and has not observed any. The militia does have access to propane and fuel from the refuge itself. Patrols are being conducted and there is a person in the watch tower 24/7 with a long rifle and radio."

He gave advice: "If the public demands they leave, CHS doesn't think the militia will leave until additional pressure is placed upon them. CHS did not know what that pressure would be, but just asking the militia to leave will not work. If the FBI continues to do nothing, the militia will just gain more people on site and more power until the FBI is forced to react. None of the core leaders have made life ending preparations at this point, but Ammon Bundy and Ryan Payne have stated they would take a bullet if needed."

There are pages and pages of these documents, and I found them incredible to read, giving as they do both a window into how the FBI deals with its informants and a picture into the minds of people who were seeing the same things I was and who were getting paid to relate their experiences and feelings, talking about people I knew. "There is no one guarding the west entrance anymore, they just have heavy equipment blocking it. The two guards at the east entrance each have an AR-15 and handgun," the report of one reads on January 7, the day

Ammon and I almost drove off to Idaho to visit his family. None of the informants seems to have picked up on that plan. "The leader of an Oregon militia group that is on site is driving a blue Dodge pickup." He's describing Brandon Rapolla's truck, which that day was parked right outside Ammon's office. He described a couple of other vehicles, and then reported on the mood: "The CHS said that rumors about an impending raid are constant and people are starting to get burned out by it."

He wrote that both Ammon and Ryan Payne had the feeling that "the majority of the townspeople are on their side, but Ammon continues to make an active effort to court the public. He is extremely charismatic and his actions like going to the barber and out to lunch before heading back to Idaho are calculated like a politician. The sense that the community is behind the occupation is exasperated [sic] by the fact that, despite several contacts, none of the occupiers have been cited by police in town.

"The tower is always manned by at least two people," he reported. "But this includes a couple that use it as a location to have sex."

The FBI seems to have been able to recruit informants across the militia and Patriot movement basically at will, reaching out to people who needed money or who happened to have encountered a criminal outside the movement who agents could use to open a discussion. But none of these people ended up testifying at trial for the prosecution—and the wild thing is that not one but two of them ended up testifying for the defense. One of these was a sort of spy-caper mercenary figure, apparently named Fabio Minoggio, who claims to have been born in Switzerland, appeared late in the standoff calling himself John Killman and speaking in a French accent, and presented himself as a weapons expert—training occupiers in team combat and hand-to-hand fighting. He seems to have regarded the whole thing as an adventure, claims not to have accepted any payment from the FBI besides compensation for his expenses, and his existence is publicly known only because he gave his phone number to someone at the refuge and one of the defense attorneys reverse-traced the number and subpoenaed him. If he thought the occupiers were doing anything wrong, his testimony doesn't make that clear.

The other informant who testified for the defense—one of three informants whose names are publicly known—became a full-on Ammon Bundy devotee. Her name is Terri Linnell, and she was a mom of two living outside San Diego. In the Patriot movement she went by the nickname Mama Bear. After she testified and her identity became public, she wrote an open letter about how she'd come up to Oregon.

She was approached in the summer of 2015 by agents working for an FBI Joint Terrorism Task Force on domestic terrorism. She said they approached asking for information about a murder suspect she says she happened to have crossed paths with, but she said that soon they made clear that they were interested in what seems to have been her rather tenuous connections to the Patriot movement. "They track local groups, such as Militia, Oathkeepers, III%, Sovereign Citizens, Black Lives Matter, Occupy, KKK, as part of their jobs," she wrote. "I was asked to go to Oath Keeper meetings and report back my thoughts on their leader. I did so. I reported he was very nice." She was given a handler, whom she called "Martha," and began to have regular meetings in a local shopping center.

She joined a III% group in her area—still reporting to the FBI—and eventually grew so involved that she was put up to be the leader of the group. Martha told her that she'd have to decline, as she couldn't keep reporting to the FBI and acting in a leadership role. She stayed in the wings.

When the occupation started, she says she begged the FBI to send her. She'd just had a brush with pneumonia, and her son had just totaled her car. "Between Christmas, the doctor bills, and the car, we were flat broke. God just was stopping me dead in my tracks," she wrote. But just as she was recovering, Martha called. "I jumped at the chance. Finally, God was letting me go!" This open letter was written as a sort of apologia to the Patriot community for acting as an informant, so it's probably worth clarifying the nature of her excitement: she was going to inform on events up there, which she did diligently, and she was going to be well paid for it. She had never met Ammon or any of the other leaders. This isn't to say she wasn't already at least somewhat sympathetic to them, but it seems impossible that her handlers would have sent her, or that she would have taken their money, if they'd had any idea of how far under Ammon's spell she would fall.

She wrote that Martha gave her $1,000 in cash, a hotel allowance of $80 a day, and a meal allowance that was "so lavish, I don't even remember the amount—it was so ridiculous."

She got to Burns on the thirteenth of January, the same day Wes and I got back to the refuge from Utah. She fell in love.

"One of the local ranchers did a big barbecue for us with all the fixings," she wrote. "I talked with him, thanking him. He had butchered a pig for us, and smoked it at home. We had a large spread of delicious cole slaw (which is the first time I ever liked cole slaw), smoked pig, and numerous other delicious foods. Everyone was there along with some other ranchers. We probably had a good 80 people come and go."

She stayed on, cooking in the bunkhouse for the crew, filing reports for Martha while she got deeper and deeper into the occupation. "I called in to Martha almost every day. Usually I just stood outside the chow hall and chatted with her," she wrote. She was asked mostly about Ammon and Ryan Bundy and Ryan Payne. "I was also asked about where the weapons were kept," she wrote. "I explained there was no stash, no warehouse, it was just people's personal weapons. I also said all weapons were legal that I saw."

She made supply runs. She kept notes on everyone, and says she eventually collected $3,000 from Martha as payment for her work as an informant. But Ammon had the same effect on her that he'd had on Shawna and LaVoy and all the rest before. She seems to have cherished her moments with him, which would make her pretty normal for the people who came to the refuge, and she herself reached out to a defense attorney, first just offering scraps of information, then making clear that she'd been an informant but wanted to help.

When she was called, she gave fawning and affectionate testimony about what she'd seen in Harney County. It took me a minute to even register how insane it was that a woman who'd taken thousands of dollars and gone up to the refuge at the FBI's behest, and kept dutifully filing her reports, could have effectively been turned into a double agent without Ammon even exerting himself. "He's the type of man who is free, unlike most," she wrote. "Most people think 'what if.' Ammon is a free man and walks this earth as a free man. He doesn't recognize fear. Anyone can disagree with Ammon, yet he'll still give them the shirt off his back if they need it, disagreeing or not."

CHAPTER 26

LaVoy

I headed back to Portland, to see my sister, rest, and buy pot and Adderall. No one seemed to question or actually to even notice it when I came back a few days later and took my usual observation chair in the little stone headquarters. It was slightly surreal—at this point, reporters were only very occasionally being allowed into the office, and even peripheral occupiers like Sean, Sandy, and Duane were kept away. I asked Duane once why I never saw him in there, and he said, "What would I do in there? That's for the important people." I was very much not important, but no one seemed to mind it much if I became an unspeaking decoration, like the dried reptiles and Indian grindstones still left on the shelves by the refuge employees who'd fled.

It was LaVoy Finicum, who up till then I'd barely even gotten to know, who first remarked on me coming back. He had a habit, when he wanted to make a point or convey excitement, of planting his legs square and spreading his arms wide, like he was getting ready to catch a hay bale. He did that, gave me a big smile, and said, "Well, where have you been? We need you around here!" It made me feel slightly queasy to try to puzzle out what he meant by this. He was wearing his cream-colored cowboy hat and a well-fitting ensemble of matching light-denim jeans and jacket, with his .45 revolver slung in a leather gun belt low on his hip. It was always hard to avoid the impression that he was having fun—dressing the cowboy part, doing wacky stuff like leading a procession of reporters ten miles down the road to climb a telephone pole and cut down an FBI surveillance camera. He, like Ammon, had an eye for spectacle and an unteachable sense of how to manufacture drama and interest. He had self-published a dystopian novel about a prepper family trying to survive a social breakdown in an apocalyptic West, and I would not be the only journalist to pick up a copy out of curiosity and to find myself forced to admit, eighty pages in, that it was a pretty fun read.

He also—very unlike Ammon—liked to reveal pieces of himself, his hopes and dreams and troubles and embarrassing little affectations, and could laugh at all of them. He claimed the spokesman role for himself, and it made sense, because he had an ability that Ammon couldn't summon to talk to strangers and non-Mormons like real people, to get away from statements of principle and to talk about his personal faith and almost adolescent love of the land and cowboy life. "It's taken me so long to live my dream of getting my own ranch," he told me. "I'm fifty-five this month and I've dreamed that dream since I was a kid, watching Roy Rogers and all that." He'd only managed to buy it six years earlier. "I finally achieved my lifelong dream," he said, "and now all that dream is put on an altar."

That June, six months after his death, LaVoy's widow,

Jeanette, called me. She was angry about a line in a piece I'd written where I quoted Steve saying that LaVoy treated Ammon like a prophet.

"My husband did not think Ammon was a prophet," she said. She was very angry. "My husband was his own man, and he made his own choices."

That may have been true, but there was something inexplicable about the esteem he had for the members of the Bundy family. He was at his place in Cane Beds, Arizona, in the "Mormon Strip" at the northern end of the state, when the showdown at the Bundy family ranch popped off. It sits at the end of a lonely dirt road choked in bright red sandstone dust. The nearest town, if you want to call it that, is Colorado City, the grim headquarters of the most famous Mormon polygamous sect.

"When I got into this I was just a rancher and a citizen of Arizona," he told me one day. "I'd watched Cliven Bundy for more than a decade. And this was the question I had: Would he fold or would he stand? I shook his hand, that was the first time I met him, and I said, 'Cliven, do not let them take your cows.' He told me to get my horse and be back in the morning, and I was the first cowboy on-site the day of the standoff." This was all it took. Almost everyone in the core of the occupation at the refuge had fallen instantly into the Bundy cause after visiting the Nevada standoff, but of them LaVoy was the only one who actually had a ranch to lose.

"I says, if Cliven was right, if the federal government has no legal or moral authority to own one-third of the landmass," he said, "then if I continue to pay my grazing fees I'm upholding something that's legally and morally wrong. And so I had to wrestle with myself.

"I says, you know, things are good for me—the range cops are good to me, their kids go do the rodeo with my kids," he went on. "But in order to have integrity within, I had to stand up and do something. That's kinda how I got thrown in here," he said. "I never intended to be embroiled in a political thing like this.

"My dream was to ranch quietly up there with my children and just to prep," he said, "and when the whole world goes under I was going to be sitting pretty because I'm out here with my cows, and my family. And now I'm one of the biggest targets in the United States—I don't know how many names you can call a person that's bad, but I think I've heard them all."

He'd been married to Jeanette for twenty-two years, and they had eleven kids and almost twenty grandchildren. She's a very sweet and, these days at least, soft-spoken woman who, when I visited, still hadn't brought herself to take down the spare gun belt looped over the mirror on his dressing table. I have trouble imagining what she must have been thinking while he was at the refuge.

I found this fucking insane. It made me actually very sad that day to see LaVoy and Ryan Bundy, grown men with wives and nineteen children between them, standing together, their revolvers propped on their hips and hats cocked back on their heads, talking casually as though their families weren't about to be ripped apart. There was something in the coincidence of my uncle and grandmother's deaths that had made me confront, in a way everyone learns to eventually, how irrevocable it all is. I was not, with the exception of Wes, what you'd call friends with anyone there. But simple proximity in a place as heated and stressful as the refuge breeds its own kind of intimacy, and while I've never had much of a problem with the idea of insurrectionary politics, I had also never really had to sit in silence for a week contemplating the reality of political violence and what horrible sadness it would work on Ammon's or LaVoy's families to see them end up dead or in prison. It made the whole thing seem selfish and silly and cruel, and then left me trying to figure out at what point I'd be willing to put my parents and sisters through what these guys were so willingly putting their families through, which at various points in the past was something I'd done mostly without thinking much about it. Maybe I was just getting older.

The amazing thing was that the grazing fees he was refusing to pay, and over which he was risking his life and ranch, were only a few thousand bucks a year. I asked if he had any other problems with the BLM, and he said not really. It was pure principle and faith in the Bundys. "I see my role as to be a defender of them," he said. "Not to be a leader. To support them in what they do."

CHAPTER 27

Foreboding

The next week was very dark. Booda, Cliven Bundy's giant tattooed and seething bodyguard, had finally come back from dealing with his warrant in Arizona, which didn't do much for the general ambience. Shawn and I were drinking late one night at the Pine Room when he showed up, looking for a hot snack before driving the rest of the way to the refuge. Bill, the owner, watched him warily, and the whole bar went quiet. Everyone knew who he was or, if they didn't, it couldn't have been hard to guess. A group of men sitting off in a corner, who one might reasonably have assumed were armed, stiffened visibly. No one, of course, doubted that Booda was armed. He sauntered past them, and after a short moment he approached the bar. He nodded grimly to us, turned to Bill, and asked for a hot chocolate. It seemed that he was really giving the Mormon thing a go.

The FBI surveillance cameras were everywhere now. The national reporters had mostly all gone home, and their rooms seemed to have been taken up by the proliferating FBI agents, their black SUVs coming and going from motel parking lots at all hours. The HRT guys were there but remained aloof even from the Oregon State Police. "I knew one that was riding with me," one OSP agent later said. "And it was hard to tell if they actually give their real names or not." He said they smirked as they introduced themselves. One of the supposed informant reports, apparently filed by the mysterious Fabio Minoggio, gives a good picture of how obvious this all was, even to bystanders: "A Safeway employee told the CHS that the town is full of Police and FBI," it reads. "The Safeway employee pointed to two male individuals in the Safeway and identified them as law enforcement. The employee advised the CHS to stay away from the Horseshoe Inn because it is filled with law enforcement."

Every morning, when I arrived at the refuge, Ammon greeted me in the same way. "Hey, nice to see you," he'd say. "What's it looking like out there, in the real world?" I kept saying it was getting darker and darker. This only provoked shrugs. "Could you verify," LaVoy asked me casually one day, "if they've taken over a wing of the hospital? A trauma unit, and brought in extra plasma and all that?" I said I had no idea. "Well, that's what they're saying on Fox News," he said, sounding unworried, and dropped the subject.

I tried to get my sense of foreboding across to both of them. This turned out to be a losing game, because no one was terribly interested in what I had to say and because they felt the foreboding too, and reveled in it. Ammon, in particular, seemed grim, but his fixity of purpose only grew as it became clearer that there was a reckoning approaching, to the point that I found it almost disturbing to talk to him. He was always outwardly friendly and measured, but he produced a sort of dark glint in his eye when he felt challenged, a look so intense and nearly malevolent that I began to avoid talking to him directly. I stayed instead as a shadow, sitting silently in the office or tailing them as they convoyed to meetings, debouching from their rigs, and swaggering in together ten deep, like a gangster's entourage.

I asked Mel Bundy, Ammon's lean and easygoing older brother, if Ammon was persuadable. He laughed at the thought. "We don't believe that Ammon talks to God directly," he said, while he waited politely for me to smoke a cigarette outside the office door. I can't imagine the look I must have given him, but he kept talking. "What we believe is that if you're living a lifestyle worthy enough to receive the inspiration of the Holy Ghost—that's what will lead you to make good decisions for the benefit of man." The point was that Ammon didn't even need to listen to the council of spirits—he knew that what he did was right by the fact that it was him doing it. We went into the office and I took my usual seat. The atmosphere inside had become so intense that it was hard to take. Shawna was whispering into her phone as I sat down. "We will keep him safe no matter what," she said, with fervor so great it seemed to strain the bounds of speech. "We will keep him safe so he can tell the world the truth."

By now their grandiosity was impossible to contain on a 187,000-acre patch of desert and marsh forty miles from town. They had replaced the sign at the gate of the refuge with a new and professional-looking sign for what they were calling the "Harney County Resource Center," and they began to come and go like they were untouchable. The Bundys went to church in Burns. LaVoy's birthday was coming up, and he was making plans for Jeanette, his wife, to visit. A whole contingent of them brazenly went to a town meeting hosted by the local county executive and held in the high school gym, where they sat in the back and loomed over the proceedings, even though they weren't allowed to speak. They hosted a packed meeting thirty miles west of Burns in Crane, where they began their plan to export their rebellion. They scheduled another meeting up the road in Grant County, where the local sheriff was an open supporter of their cause. The sheriff was going to cohost the meeting. It says something about the swell of events that it didn't even seem strange to me that an elected sheriff would host a meeting for a group of America's most famous outlaws. Ammon reached out to the FBI, supposedly to open negotiations, but he did it in person—rolling up to the airport in force and talking to the negotiator by phone, while the FBI agents beyond looked like they were getting ready to invade Crimea. It was pointless—he could have called from the refuge, and anyway he never gave any serious indication that he really wanted to negotiate. But it was great theater, it made him look fearless, and it kept them in the news. Ammon understood, maybe better than any of us watching him did yet, that we were all living in a time and place where the difference between politics and theater had collapsed, and where presenting yourself as fearlessly "making a hard stand," as he always put it, could make you a hero even to people who had no idea of what you actually stood for. He reportedly said he was done talked to Harney County officials and that it was time for them to "get in line."

One afternoon I walked over to the stables to visit Hellboy

and was surprised to find a young black guy named Brandon helping Duane to muck out the stalls. He was from Pine Bluff, Arkansas, and obsessed with futurist schemes of vertical farms and geothermal energy. He was deliberately polite and soft-spoken and called everyone "sir." It was hard to understand why he was there. I had once been picked up by a sheriff's deputy while trying to hitchhike through Pine Bluff, and so we talked for a while about how it was a rough town. We went into a side building that had once been used as a museum and he introduced me to David Fry, a half-Japanese and half-cocked young guy with a faint mustache and long black hair who had set up a livestreaming command center. The tough-guy contingent didn't like him, and Ryan Payne had actually tried to make him leave, but LaVoy felt bad for him and had let him set up in the side building. "You want some of this?" he asked me, holding up a pipe and some pot, and they smoked in full view of LaVoy, who seemed unable to identify the smell. David was from outside of Cincinnati, and so we talked about home, which seemed a long way away. He had been in and out of mental facilities as a teenager, and had pretty severe para-noid tendencies, which had coalesced after a string of arrests for pot possession into a sense that the government was out to get him. He spent his time at home obsessively playing World of Tanks, researching conspiracy theories, and looking for companionship in his quest to expose government tyranny, which is how he began e-mailing with LaVoy, who invited him out and became his sponsor on the refuge. His parents, who were worried senseless, called him every day. It was ludicrous and infuriating that they were there, a pair of nerdy lost boys, who couldn't have given the barest sketch of what the core occupiers believed, smoking pot and looking at Wikipedia pages on techno-utopian schemes together, in the time they had left over from carrying a rifle and standing on the front lines in the war to restore a lost nation they'd never known. It later turned out that Brandon had an outstanding warrant from Kansas, for stealing a gun. Fry ended up being the last occupier to surrender.

I declined to smoke weed with them. I excused myself and caught LaVoy as he was coming out. "I need an hour with Ammon today," I told him.

He looked slightly affronted and bemused, like I'd misunderstood my role there and now was overstepping. "Well, you know Ammon's always busy," he said. "I'm not even sure where he is." I said I could wait.

"Why don't you talk to me?" he said. "We can go to my office right now, actually." I said we could do that too, but that I'd still be wanting to talk to Ammon. He paused. "What do you need to talk to him about?" he asked, and I said, somewhat to my own surprise, that I'd decided to leave, that I wanted a final sit-down, and that I was sure Ammon would find some time for it. He said he'd set it up.

I felt a wild need to confront him. I'd been forming a set of thoughts over the course of the week. It started, in a way I still find embarrassing and uncomfortable to talk about, with a sort of spiritual awakening. I had never thought that I had a religion, but there was something about the feel of the experience on the refuge, the sense that so much of it had already been written, and the indescribable intensity of instantly formed relationships, and the odd wild comfort and communion I felt with the land and the plants around me that in some strange way I had stopped doubting that Ammon was talking to or being guided by something beyond human motivation.

I didn't become Christian, but in the next few months I found myself being surprised at how moved I was by the old mountain hymns from home, about the power in the blood and the old country church and things like that, and on some level I found this a balm for the far more embarrassing and uncomfortable fact of how drawn to and impressed by Ammon I'd been—because if he was really talking to spirits, then I could hardly blame myself for being compelled by him. I'm not trying to convince anyone here—it's just where I was coming from.

And then I was standing in the snow, talking to a man I liked pretty well and who I was sure would soon be dead—in the name of a cause that Ammon, at least, was surely smart enough to know couldn't be won. There was no doubt that Ammon alone had the power to avoid whatever reckoning was coming. We went to find him, after talking for a while in LaVoy's office about his kids and his childhood growing up on the Navajo reservation and the foster kids he and Jeanette hosted on the ranch, before this had caused the state to order them removed. I tried to press him on how he could get so wrapped up in the Bundy cause so quickly, and I guess I tried, without really having the guts to say it, to convey how badly I thought he'd been cheated by people who'd sold him a line about this whole cause being about standing up for the little guy. And by a man who didn't seem to really care what happened to his family, or all of their families, or whether or not he was even going to live or die. He laughed me off. "You know, there aren't any leaders here," he said. "We all make our own choices. We're just brothers." He paused. "We're brothers in the cause of freedom."

I don't think he wanted to die, but I knew then that he thought that was where things were headed. He took me over to Ammon's office. Booda stood by, glowering and impatient, with Blaine Cooper sitting next to Ammon, looking bored and annoyed. Ammon sat next to me. It was the coldest encounter I'd had on the refuge. He talked to me like a stranger and like, at a certain point, if I hadn't got the truth of what he was doing and why they were there, that I was beyond help and wasting his time.

It's strange to talk about this now, because it sounds crazy and I can't quite recapture the feeling, but in that moment I felt hate wash over me. It felt refreshing. This had to do with my new little spiritual awakening, which had got me thinking about evil and whether it wasn't possible that there was such a force in the world. I figured that if there was, it was probably whatever force made some terrorist or mad dictator feel the impetus of his own cause to the point that he loses touch with basic human decency. And I'd always thought—maybe wrongly, but before I would have been unable to talk without red-eared embarrassment about any spiritual feelings—that there was some basic part of the American spirit that tended to resist this sort of thinking, that we might have more than our share of hate and blindness but that there was something innate to the American mind that rejected murderous, divisive certitudes.

There was something about seeing how quickly, in his presence, decent-seeming people I enjoyed talking to could start thinking about becoming martyrs, how a county where everyone seemed to know one another could be brought so easily into a place of almost irreconcilable division, how so many people across the West and across the nation could turn him into a hero without having any real sense of him at all—just because he showed them a front of otherworldly certitude—that made me think that this evil was being actively loosed on the land, and that Ammon, for all his gentle talk, had become its willing agent. I feel this way about the oligarchs who have fed all this hate and division in the West, and I feel it about the cabal that now runs our country, but I'd never had them sitting in front of me, and there Ammon was. He had such a strange flash in his eye during those weeks. I did not doubt that he was guided by some force beyond human reckoning. I just didn't think it was the Holy Spirit. I thought it might have been the devil. I had never had any thoughts like this before.

I felt off balance. I asked, for the thousandth time, why people were so quick to follow him. "We all understand that there is a supreme being," he said. "You've probably experienced that we pray all the time." I said that I'd even prayed with them. "Right," he said. "And there might be someone who says the prayer different, but we all know we're praying to the same being, and there's that respect and love that comes from that.

"The Lord has no respect for a person," he said. "Blaine here settin' next to us, he has a function and a purpose, and he does that."

Blaine didn't say anything. "And then there were a series of things, mostly a desire to learn and get educated, and get your bearings right," he went on, "so you can do what you're supposed to do. And each person here is doing that." This was what bothered me so much—this idea that there was some kind of learnably correct way to be an American.

"We're like ISIS or whatever, but American," Blaine had said earlier, shrugging. "I guess you could call us constitutional extremists."

We talked for half an hour. I'd kept circling back over the course of the week to the thought that Ammon would probably be in prison, if he was even still living, at the time his kids started graduating from high school. This thought infuriated me for some reason. I brought it up. It's almost impossible to convey in writing how cold he was. He spoke with a note of derision that couldn't be missed but that was too gentle to sound like anger, like a parent talking to a kid who's just been caught cheating on a test. "My family, my wife, my children, and those around us believe that you do what's right," he said, the clear implication being that if I didn't share their strength of conviction then that was something I could examine on my own time. "You do what is right, and you do what you're supposed to do, and you let the consequence follow. And that's what we're doing." I looked at him for a moment, and then stuck out my hand and we shook.

"I want to say good luck," I said. He shrugged. "Not for, like, all this—but just, I don't know . . . I hope everyone comes out okay." We shook hands and he thanked me, with a look that said he didn't much think he needed my good wishes. I was surprised and a bit ashamed at how much this hurt me.

CHAPTER 28

Put the Bullet
Through Me

This is how things ended.

Ammon rode in an orange Jeep toward the meeting in John Day. He was unarmed and carrying $8,031 in cash on him. Booda sat with him in the back, and an FBI informant named Mark McConnell drove. In front of the Jeep, LaVoy was driving his big white diesel Dodge Ram crew cab, with Arizona plates and a cap over the bed. It was the day before his fifty-fifth birthday. Ryan Payne sat in the passenger seat. Behind him was Shawna Cox, and behind LaVoy sat Ryan Bundy. In between them was an eighteen-year-old gospel singer named Victoria Sharp, who was supposed to perform for the meeting that night with her seven younger siblings, in a group they called the Sharp Family Singers.

They drove north from Burns up US 395, which quickly rose into a low, brushy canyon dotted with junipers, following the course of a snow-fed waterway called Poison Creek. After fifteen miles they crossed into the Malheur National Forest. They lost cell service as they climbed and the junipers began to be replaced with broad ponderosas, tall enough to darken the road. "That's when we got a bad feeling," Shawna told me later, "when we lost coverage in the mountains." The plan was to solidify and spread their rebellion to Grant County, after the meetings with Harney County ranchers at the refuge and up in Crane, and after sympathetic meetings, one of which had been organized by Todd and funded by old Bert Smith, in which ranchers in Utah and Idaho signed papers committing themselves to refuse contracts with the federal government. They knew that a trip so far from the refuge was a risk, but Ammon viewed it as an important next step, and they had reason to believe they would be safe from arrest in John Day—the sheriff, an angry constitutionalist named Glenn Palmer who would soon be narrowly reelected, was, after all, as much a Bundyite as anyone.

"I knew going into it that there was a sheriff in Grant County that was supporting the movement or the ideology behind what they were pushing," an Oregon State Police officer later told investigators. "I knew that there was a large amount of community members in Grant County that supported their beliefs . . . that for a very simple way to put it, they were not friendly to law enforcement conducting any enforcement actions, and mainly the Federal Bureau of Investigation and federal agencies."

The OSP said, maybe not fully truthfully, that they learned about the John Day meeting by reading about it in the newspaper. The day before they convened in Bend to plan the stop. Officers would later describe themselves as sleeping very well that night. They arrived at the command post at the airport outside Burns. They were worried that occupiers were watching their movements, and so they rolled out in staggered deployments. They were unsure what side Palmer's department would take in any confrontation, and so they positioned themselves well inside the Harney County line at a roadside snowmobiling park unmarked even on high-detail maps.

The rest of the Sharp family, traveling ahead of Ammon and LaVoy, had passed a group of unmarked cars and had tried to call back and warn them, but the call wouldn't go through. A plane overhead was tracking their movements and relaying their location to two groups, both composed of officers from the OSP SWAT team and from the FBI's Hostage Rescue Team. The first group was at the roadside sno-park; the second was half a mile down the road at a horse camp, ready to put up a roadblock. Three vehicles pulled out as Ammon and LaVoy passed. "We all turned our lights on," an officer who in later investigations would be identified only as Officer 2 later said. "The Jeep Wrangler immediately slowed and stopped without any incident whatsoever." It was, after all, being driven by an informant. Ammon and Booda were arrested.

LaVoy kept going and drove forward a few yards before stopping in the middle of the road. "So initially there was two conversations going on," Officer 2 remembered. Everyone was shouting. Ryan Payne was talking to FBI agents on the passenger side of the vehicle, while LaVoy yelled at OSP officers from the driver's side window. "Payne acts like—he's kind of half out of the truck," Officer 2 said. "He starts to kind of go back in, and Officer No. 5 fires a 40 millimeter less lethal sponge tip round which hits him in the arm." Payne, after some shouting and dissimulating, put his hands up and surrendered.

This left LaVoy in the driver's seat of his truck, with Shawna, young Victoria Sharp, and Ryan Bundy all on the bench seat in the back. Shawna was filming on the little digital camera she carries everywhere with her. LaVoy put his hands out the window. "The sheriff is waiting for us," he yelled out toward an OSP officer known in later reports as Officer 4. "So you do as you damn well please. Here I am," he said, and indicated some part of his body. "Right there, and you can put a bullet through it."

Officer 4 may have said something in response, or maybe LaVoy just continued unprompted. "Do you understand? I'm going to meet the sheriff. You can back down, or kill me now. Go ahead, put the bullet through me. I'm going to meet the sheriff. You can do as you damn well please."

Officer 4 shouted something about getting the women out of the truck. "What for?" Shawna said, her voice no more agitated than it sounded months later, when I heard her telling her grandson to go read a book.

"Who are you?" Ryan Bundy bellowed out, until someone called back that they were from the Oregon State Police. "Well I'm going to go meet the sheriff in Grant County," LaVoy shouted back. "You can come along with us, and you can talk with us over there." When Officer 4 didn't seem amenable to this idea, LaVoy indicated his forehead. "You can put the laser right there," he said, "and put the bullet through my head. Okay boys? It's going to get real. You want my blood on your hands, then get it done," he said. "Because we've got people to see and places to go."

For some reason LaVoy reached over and turned up the radio. A pop station came on. The words "We hold each other, we hold each other" filled the truck cab. "Who can we call?" Ryan asked.

"Call Joseph Rice," Shawna said.

"We got people en route," LaVoy shouted out. The idea was that if they could get to Joseph, the PPN militias in Burns would have only fifteen miles to travel. There was no question that the PPN in full force would have outgunned the arrest team at the sno-park. They scrambled to find his number. There wasn't any service.

"We should never have stopped," Ryan said.

"I'm gonna keep going," LaVoy said. "Ready?"

"Well, where's those guns?" Ryan asked. LaVoy repeated that he was going. "Okay, then get down," Shawna said to the rest of them in the backseat, and she lay over Victoria while LaVoy hit the gas on the diesel. They were quickly doing seventy.

Officer 2 got back in his truck and followed. They traveled half a mile and rounded a curve. There was a three-car road-block, as police would later put it, "approximately 862 feet away" from them as they hit the turn. LaVoy either froze and couldn't react or decided to try to blow past it. "Hang on," Ryan called out. "They're shooting," Shawna said quietly. LaVoy said nothing as his truck closed the distance. An OSP officer, later identified as Officer 1, watched the approach and, it seems, coolly put three rounds into the truck as it approached.

The first one hit a side-view mirror, another hit the radiator, and the third hit the hood above a headlight. The truck dove into a three-foot snowbank and kept traveling for 105 feet, missing a fleeing FBI agent by an actual matter of inches. I have no idea what LaVoy's plan was at this point. Within seconds he was out of the truck. "Go ahead and shoot me," he yelled, putting his hands fully up and in view. An FBI HRT agent fired two quick rounds immediately after these words. It's not clear why he was firing, but one round hit the truck and broke a passenger window, and one round seems to have flown off into the distance. LaVoy's hands were clearly up at this point. The agent supposed to have fired these shots was later indicted in federal court for lying in an attempt to obstruct justice, after he allegedly lied to investigators, and tried to cover up the fact that he'd fired. His shell casings disappeared.

LaVoy still held his hands out and far apart, the same catching-a-hay-bale gesture he always made. He turned around—a full, awkward pirouette in the snow—which would have given him a view of Officers 1 and 2, each with rifles trained at him. Officers ordered him to get down, and he kept shouting. "You're going to have to shoot me, just go ahead and shoot me." Victoria Sharp screamed wildly, and then went quiet. "Stay down," Shawna told her.

There were now three officers near him. He was in a snowbank on the west side of the road, and he stood facing north. He left Officers 1 and 2 behind him and turned his attention to Officer 3, who was approaching from the timberline on the west side of the road, a Taser held out in his left hand.

Both Officers 1 and 2 later described fearing for the safety of Officer 3. "As I stepped up and was moving," Officer 2 told it, "I saw Mr. Finicum turn his back toward me and Officer 1, and then I saw his right arm again dig deeply in toward what I would term as maybe a shoulder holster or something."

LaVoy seemed to jerk with his right hand toward his left. In a jacket pocket on that side, according to reports, was a loaded 9mm semiautomatic given to him by his stepson. "And just as soon as I pulled my rifle up and put it on Mr. Finicum, Officer 1 fired, and I heard him fire, and I knew it was him firing, for whatever reason. And as soon as he fired and my scope just came up and was right in the middle of the back of Mr. Finicum and I squeezed off a single round." Three rounds, from two different rifles, hit LaVoy from behind.

"Damn it," Shawna said. "Are they shooting him? Did they shoot him?" She paused. "You assholes."

"Oh my god," Victoria said. "Is he dead?" Then she began to really scream, the wild incoherent screams of a teenage girl who had held it together pretty well through all of this and was now realizing that she'd just seen a man killed and that she had no idea if she herself was going to make it out of the dead man's truck alive. The OSP officers began firing gas rounds and flashbangs. Victoria screamed louder. "Shut up," Shawna told her. "Stay down." A gas round exploded. "Oh, shit," Shawna said.

"Did they kill him?" Victoria asked softly.

"I think they did," Shawna said. A foam-tipped round hit a

window but didn't break it. "Aw, shit, quit shooting our windows!" she said.

"God keep us safe, please," Victoria said softly, and Shawna began to lead a prayer. "Please protect us," she said, and repeated it three more times. "We need help, we need help, we need help."

CHAPTER 29

Home to Glory

I can't remember who called me first. I think it was Todd. "So you probably know what I know," he said. After the trip to Salt Lake our phones had begun doing a funny thing. He would call, and then after a moment the call would be interrupted by another call from his same number. If I declined that call, and remained on the original call, then nothing worked and we had to go back to square one. If I accepted the new call everything worked fine. It may have been that we just had a month of weird connections, but it had us both on edge. "They said there was one person shot," he said. "I think we have an idea of who that would be." I don't have notes on the call, but I remember that it wasn't very long, because there wasn't much to say. Todd signed off to call Jeanette, LaVoy's now widow. I called Jason Patrick, who was about to be put in charge down at the refuge. "People are always saying rumors and everything else," he said. "Right now I'm not going anywhere and not believing anything I can't verify. Pretty soon I'm going to go to sleep."

It was becoming a frantic night. When I started getting calls I was on the balcony of a borrowed condo in a retirement community in Florida, trying to write a eulogy for my uncle, whose service was going to be in two days. I was already slightly undone and was drinking so much rum—it was Florida—that bottles began to fill up the condo and I was slightly frayed every afternoon when I woke up and went to see my parents, my sister, and my baby niece, who were all down for the memorial. I was crying a lot and missed Uncle Reppie, who had left Cincinnati when I was still a kid. He'd had a wife and a career and a big house at one point, and I'd never been fully sure what he was fleeing from when he left home in the wake of the marriage and washed up, eventually, on Singer Island, where he spent the last fifteen years of his life living alone save for his dog—a needy little fuzzball called Edgar Allan Pogue—and making a living renting out beach chairs and umbrellas to the various retirees who populated the beach, year in and year out. I had only ever visited him once, when I was eighteen and on vacation with my then girlfriend, but we were close in a way that was hard to put—both big talkers who got each other without ever having to push too hard against the midwestern bounds that circumscribed our intimate worlds, and we both liked girls and to sit out on a porch talking shit and to have a drink or six, though he'd quit long ago and replaced it with a case-a-day Diet Pepsi habit. He was five foot four and walked with a limp from a bad hip, and still dressed like a certain sort of Cincinnatian, though he barely had enough money to pull it off anymore—battered blue blazers and Brooks Brothers khakis and sockless penny loafers. He had a blind devotion to Jen, and they shared an easy closeness that really none of us could ever match, a constant joking bickering that made her seem very different—softer—in his presence. I always imagined him as very lonely down in Florida without her. I had always thought that someday I'd go down and spend a week or more with him and just talk and get from him the family stories I felt strange talking to my mother about and maybe selfishly to see what his reason for running off had been and if it was something I could learn from for myself. And suddenly in the juxtaposition of his death against all these close Mormon families I'd been dealing with, I felt an unanswerable sadness and weird anger directed at more or less all the forces in American life that had made it possible or normal to live so far away from and in such superficial contact with the people who matter most to you, and then at Ammon, who had gone so willingly to Harney County and perverted their desire to retain order and meaning in their way of life into his stupid pageant of violence, and now this man who I had liked, to be honest, pretty well had been shot over really nothing at all, and somehow the confluence of their deaths seemed significant, if only to me, and like quite a lot to take.

It was about ten p.m. I ate some Ritalin and smoked cigarettes on the balcony. Wes called. When I picked up, the same thing happened with our phones that had when Todd called. He seemed undone, unclear who he was even angry at. "The thing about it, man," he said, "is that it's so frustrating when you have a fucking cause and you become absolutist. I was there—but I fucking recognize reality, man. This didn't need to fucking happen.

"These guys are not fucking scared, man, that's what you

have to understand. And like, I think what they're doing is right, but these people are fucking extreme, man. It didn't need to turn into this."

I said that I thought on some level it really had needed to turn into this, that this had been the whole point. This is where the moderate, confused, curious version of Wes that I'd first known began for a time to fade away.

"I already said that I was trying to be levelheaded," he said, "and if shots were fired, I'd fucking lie down. But now, what? They would have probably just fucking killed me too." The story of LaVoy's death being a government assassination was already taking hold, and it didn't help at all when later it emerged that at least some portion of the HRT team had actually, literally, engaged in a cover-up. I didn't believe LaVoy was murdered and still don't, but it was hard to know what to think.

At the moment, Ammon, Booda, Victoria Sharp, Ryan Payne, Ryan Bundy, and Shawna were speeding in a convoy of SUVs toward Portland. "I don't know if they were going eighty or ninety or what," Shawna told me. "But they were going fast, and they didn't stop for anything, not any red lights or anything. They just blew through the middle of Bend. I thought they were going to kill someone." Somehow, Ammon still had a phone on him, and he managed, with his cuffs on, to make a call to Lisa. An officer eventually found the phone shoved down in a crack in the backseat. Victoria Sharp asked four times to be allowed to go to the bathroom. These requests were ignored or refused. Eventually she could hold it no longer and finished the six-hour ride in urine-soaked pants. She was never officially arrested. "I was just worried about her," Shawna said. "I hadn't done anything wrong. I mean, none of us had. But I was just trying to be a mother."

Things suddenly seemed to be happening inexplicably quickly. Wes went unhinged. A rumor spread that indictments were coming down for everyone who'd been at the Sugar Pine and the original Nevada standoff. Two days later I gave a very dark speech for Reppie's memorial, in which I said that I'd been experiencing a beginner's course in death and loss those past few months and that somehow talking to all his friends and discovering his world down there had given me to think that he wasn't as dead as he'd seemed a week before. "At least you spoke from the heart," an old man came up to say to me afterward. I wrote a short piece for the *New York Times Magazine* about the refuge, which was met with a universally negative stream of comments from liberals arguing more or less that I was an ignorant terrorist sympathizer blindly enamored of cowboys and that LaVoy was a violent monster who got what he deserved—which made me sad just because it was astonishing to see how much true hatred and loathing could be summoned toward these people who I thought, if nothing else, were human and complicated like anybody. My editors and I had earnestly thought that showing the human and complicated side of things wasn't the same as offering a defense, but that kind of thinking belonged to a time before 2016.

I went back to New York. The FBI had sealed the roads to the refuge. Some people turned themselves in. Jason hiked five miles through the desert up past an FBI checkpoint, but they got him anyway. They even arrested Hellboy and kept him in a stable up in Deschutes County. I wrote a longer piece for the *Times Magazine*. It was liked well enough that Shawn was sent back to Burns to get shots for a cover photo. Wes went back to Burns to join a PPN protest against the FBI, and they met each other there. He wore a black cowboy hat and sunglasses and shouted deliriously about an FBI cover-up. "Who is that guy?" one reporter asked Shawn. "Is he on drugs?"

Jen finally began to slip away. I got a call from my mom saying she wouldn't live through the night, that same day the *Times* asked me to go back to Burns to report one final scene. I had been planning to go to Cincinnati and be there as she died. My family all said I should go to Burns. I dithered. She died. The next day the brain trust at the *Times* decided that the moment for a story about the refuge might have passed, and the story was spiked.

My editor, who was still doggedly trying to find a way to get the piece in the magazine, asked me jokingly if I was going to kill myself, and I took the question seriously and gave him an earnest and involved answer as to why I didn't plan on it. It was an awkward moment. The only holdouts at the refuge now were a guy I'd never met named Jeff Wayne Banta, Sean and Sandy Anderson, and David Fry. Fry livestreamed an absurd and painful-to-watch drama as the FBI closed in. Banta basically said nothing, and later it came out that he stuck around less out of defiance than because he was confused about how to extricate himself without being shot, which is what Sean, Sandy, and David were convinced would happen if the government had its way. Sean and Sandy babbled in their Wisconsin accents about Waco. David, whose defining traits were a tender sensibility and a severe strain of dissociative paranoia, shook loose from reality, and Sean and Sandy fed off his fear and exacerbated it with their learned brand of black-helicopter terror of federal thugs, until they were all a screaming mess, sitting there surrounded in a tent in the snow shouting, "Just kill us now," while thousands of people followed live. I listened all night as they debated whether to live or die. Banta surrendered in the morning and then Sean and Sandy followed, after Franklin Graham and Michele Fiore—a former Nevada state representative and a longtime disciple of the Bundys—showed up, and finally David was left there alone in the tent with a rifle, he said, pointed at his head. And not to endorse what happened at the refuge, but he'll always be an American hero to me for how he surrendered. For hours it had seemed inevitable that he'd kill himself, and he sounded as if he were drifting further and further from sanity, yelling that he'd been denied pot and about crazy conspiracies and generally sounding totally unreachable by the FBI negotiators. I was so sure he was going to kill himself that I almost closed the livestream, thinking that I didn't want to be one of the people who listened while this sad, lost boy lived out LaVoy's and Ammon's whole death-before-surrender creed more actively than either of them had. And then suddenly he had a moment of clarity. "They're going to at least say a hallelujah," he said. I thought he was kidding or had just gone so crazy that he was saying random words. But the negotiators quickly confirmed that the FBI agents would be willing to say whatever he wanted, so long as he came out peacefully. "Okay," he said. "I'm going to get a cookie, and one more cigarette." This done, he stepped out and let himself be arrested, while dozens of FBI agents shouted, "Hallelujah, hallelujah, hallelujah." This was the official end.

Wes was arrested in Utah, while driving his five-ton camo military truck with a fifty-three-foot trailer hitched to the back. "Dude, you can't imagine," he said. "I'm like by the side of the road and *all* these cops are like, 'Get the fuck down, get the fuck down! If you don't do *exactly* as we say we'll shoot you.' They had rifles to the back of my head and shit, and I'm like, *okay, okay, dang.*"

I bought a new 4x4 and took to driving around Brooklyn with an illegal shotgun in the back just for the feel it gave me. They moved Wes to pretrial detention in Nevada. I quit smoking. The FBI arrested Dave and Mel Bundy, E. J. Parker, who had been with us at the Sugar Pine, and Jerry Delemus, the guy from the Trump campaign, and fifteen other people on charges over the Nevada standoff.

Then I was on the phone with the media guy from the law firm representing Ammon. We'd been talking so I could settle a few fact-checking questions, and one day he said, offhand, "You know, Ammon would like to talk." I asked what this meant exactly, and he said, "Oh, I mean in person. Ammon would like for you to come." I wrote this last sentence down, because it pissed me off. I have no idea what Ammon's personal words actually were, or even if he said anything at all or if the media guy was just trying to gin up an interview, but there was something typical of the prophet side of him in the phrasing, and typical of him that he'd suggest without apology that I go all the way to Portland to spend two hours in jail with someone who had already in some way taken over my life, and not exactly for the better, and had got LaVoy killed and had got Wes, with whom I felt extremely close and somewhat responsible for, put in jail now facing a decade or more in prison. The whole idea felt doubly absurd because there seemed to be nothing to talk about, besides maybe to ask if he thought that getting LaVoy killed and twenty-six other people thrown in jail and having twenty-six families thrown into fear and apprehension for the future had been worth it. Then I thought some more, and decided that asking him that question might be a perfectly good reason to go to Portland. So I loaded up the new rig and drove west.

CHAPTER 30

Freedomland

It took months to get clearance for the jail visit. I went to Cincinnati for my Jen's funeral. I met my buddy Dan, who had just lost a job and was at a similarly low, lost, and drunk point in his existence, and we spent a week buying guns and gear and customizing the new rig, a 2002 Toyota 4Runner that I'd got cheap because it had a big dent in the tailgate, and which soon had a three-inch lift kit, and hand-painted black wheels and big off-roading tires and a safari rack. Wes, Jon, and Steve had been initiating me into the western obsession with built-out trucks and off-roading, and though it's a little embarrassing to admit, I had become slightly consumed with building out a vehicle that could be both like something I'd own and that redneck guys would regard as legit. Growing up in southwestern Ohio, so close to the front lines of our politico-cultural wars, has always made me maybe a bit oversensitive to the not very subtle implications from right-wing men in our neighborhood that being of the left or caring about the environment was somehow incompatible with their idea of masculinity. Being in the West had only heightened this sense, with all the times some militiaman or guy at a bar would say to me, "You're not like, you know, how most liberal guys are," as though they had never really considered the possibility that someone they weren't immediately sure they could beat up might also care about how cops treat black people or think that it made sense for the Environmental Protection Agency to exist. There's a part of me that knows that it's silly to get caught up in this sort of thing, but I also think it can't be overstated how many men in this country have been conned into equating a psycho brand of right-wing politics with American masculinity in general, and every once in a while, sitting around at a bar in Texas and hearing people talk about "that pussy Obama" or whatever, I have felt consumed by a desire to knock a guy off his stool just to let him stew for a bit about what it feels like to get beat down by an effete leftist. Nowadays, of course, this doesn't seem like a particularly radical thing to think. I had always loved big trucks and guns, and had mostly until then just never had the time, money, or need to buy the iterations of both that I'd always wanted—but still the rig, and the cruel-looking, short-barreled, tactical pump-action we threw in the back of it, became my own sort of private fuck-you to every hateful guy in camo I'd ever met who figured that he was more man than I was because I have tattoos and I don't wear my jeans three sizes too big.

We camped for a week in West Texas, in a favorite spot of mine right on the Rio Grande, and then cut up to the Gila National Forest, in southwestern New Mexico. That forest happens to encompass the Gila Wilderness, which in 1924 became the first wilderness area so designated in the country. Somewhere in its dry fastnesses, up near the headwaters of the

Gila River, is the spot where Geronimo, my first great boyhood hero and a figure I still identify with sort of obsessively, was born. Those were the reasons I wanted to go there in particular, but in Texas we'd been at Big Bend National Park, and I also wanted Dan to see what it was like to be on real public lands, where you weren't stuck with all the permits and time limits and crowds of old vacationers in their $60,000 RVs and annoying visits from nosy volunteer rangers that come with staying even in a park like Big Bend, which is one of the least-trafficked parks in the country. I'm glad the Parks Service exists, and I don't begrudge its right to do what's needed to let people come and visit—which is to try to facilitate access for all the millions of casual travelers who come, while trying to be rigorously preservationist at the same time. This is a very difficult line to walk, and it means that there are rules and regulations for just about every fucking thing you can do and that by necessity it is very difficult to interact with the land in any way that doesn't involve simply walking through it and observing, down to the point that you can't let your dog run or discharge a firearm or take home a pebble or feather as a souvenir, all of which makes sense if you think about the millions upon millions of people who visit national parks every year. There are admonitions all over Big Bend, saying that if everyone who came took a pebble home, soon there wouldn't be any pebbles left at all. Still, they feel to me like outdoor hotels.

We spent a day in Silver City, New Mexico. In a junk store we happened to meet a couple of beautiful trainhopper girls who had just been thrown out of a café because they smelled too ripe, and I got to talking to them about hitchhiking in the area and what freight trains they'd been riding, because I'd come through this way when I first started hoboing nine years before, just a few weeks after I'd ridden with the border-vigilante trucker. They told us they'd been living for a couple of weeks in a cave in the national forest, somewhere up near a hot spring, which we resolved to try to find but then forgot the name of. We drove up into the mountains and stopped to pick up a map at a ranger station heading into the forest. The guy behind the desk was about our age, the sort of local who likes to describe himself as "Mexican" because his family had been there longer than the United States has existed. It was the first weekend of turkey season, and we asked him for tips on secluded spots. He gave us some tips, and I asked what permits we needed to fill out to camp up in the forest. He thought this was funny.

"No, bro, you guys are good," he said.

I asked if there was a limit on how long we could stay. "I mean, you aren't gonna live up there, are you?" he said. "It's not gonna be an issue."

I asked if we needed a fire permit. "Nah, bro," he said. I asked if we could pop the gun out to practice shooting. We had clays in the truck and a sling to throw them. "Yeah, why not?" he said. He gave us tips on spots to fly-fish and suggestions on easy spots to find water if we ran out at the campsite and needed to filter some. "There's really not that much you can do up there that I'm going to care about," he said. This here was one of our tyrannical land managers, stealing the West from the common man.

"Wait," Dan said when we were back in the truck. "That dude said we can do basically whatever we want up there." It was phrased as a statement, but it came out more like a question. I told him he was having the same reaction that I'd had when I first started to realize what the term "public lands" really meant, and we headed up toward the mesa.

We set the odometer when we left the pavement, and we were about thirty miles back on Forest Service roads when we found a campsite we liked. It was about half a mile of fairly hard 4x4 driving from the main dirt road, a big shady expanse of soft, flat ground encircled by huge ponderosas. There was no one around for miles, and we set up camp and sang and danced in our underwear and ran off to blast the gun at nothing in particular and drove around on old, barely there roads that obviously hadn't been driven in ages, crashing the truck over big trees fallen over the path just because we could, and we generally acted like giddy lunatics. "It's Freedomland," Dan said, and that became the campsite name. "We live here forever and we're never leaving and we're the kings of the mountains."

In sunny spots the lupine had begun to bloom, big purple cones of pea flowers rising a foot and a half high, in defiance of the nightly frost that had us sleeping cuddled up together in a tent far too small for two grown men. We drove forty more miles up into the forest to fly-fish at the tiny headwaters of the Gila and to be near whatever spot Geronimo had been born. Dan caught nine trout and released them all. I only had a couple of strikes, but I got to collect wildflowers and a couple of species of artemisia I'd never seen, and I found a beautiful piece of chalcedony and a chunk of porous volcanic rock filled with big fat zeolites, a delicate sort of crystal formed by water filtering into rock cavities. So I was only mildly furious. "Dude," Dan said. "Listen, you did good. Sometimes getting skunked doesn't mean you're a bad fisherman."

This is an easy thing to say when you aren't actually a bad fisherman. I realized I was mad and said I needed to stop the car for a minute. I went off alone with the gun and shot off five rounds and thought about some things and listened to the shots echo through the canyons and tramped around in the brush and soon felt great again. "Honestly, I was freaking out," he told me later. "I thought you had killed yourself." I may have been in a rougher emotional condition than I realized. We had fished too long, and night fell while I was having my private moment, so we drove back in the dark over the forty miles of bad-to-nonexistent roads, dodging coyotes and jackrabbits and skidding through streambeds and singing along to the radio. We didn't encounter signs of a single human on that drive.

I'm relating this not because it was a great adventure but because it was something both of us needed right at that time. We were pretty much clean and sober for a couple of weeks, with the exception of a bag of coke I found in a jacket pocket, which we had to do before we hit the Border Patrol checkpoints on I-10, and we rebuilt our friendship and smoothed our frayed nerves and forgot to think about things for a while. We knew we were going to come down off the mesa soon, because we had girls to see in Santa Fe and meetings to have in LA and Dan would eventually run out of cigarettes and presumably our mothers would want to know how we were doing, but we also knew that on some level we didn't have to—that the nights were only going to get warmer, and that it was still pretty much too cold and early for good trout fishing, and that with a quick trip to the store for a supply of beans and tortillas we could live up there all spring and summer, if not longer.

This, to me, is what it means to have public lands. That a third of our landmass exists as a potential Freedomland for any of us who develops a need to go and find it. That we as a people hold and manage lands in trust for me and for ranchers and for a girl who might arrive in New York from Bangladesh tomorrow—and might not even have a chance or a desire to go west in her lifetime but might still want to pass this collective inheritance down to her children. That we manage them, imperfectly, according to the needs of all of us. I think these lands color our sense of ourselves as Americans, no matter if we ever put them to the "productive use" that the Patriots obsess over. I can do okay, in short doses, living in the circus of rules that is New York City—but I would hate to live in a country where getting out on the land meant having to be in a space as heavily regulated as a national park. I don't currently plan on becoming a wild-bearded old miner working a placer claim on some lonely creek, but I would hate to live in a country where that wasn't an option if I fuck everything else up. My arsenal of firearms right now is nothing very warlike, but I would hate to live in country without wild mountain fastnesses "to function as bases for guerrilla warfare against tyranny," as Ed Abbey put it long ago. Environmentalists can think these kinds of thoughts too. Sharing a part of these lands shaped my conception of myself long before I ever set foot on the lands themselves. They gave me a sense of possibility far beyond the bounds of my immediate existence.

This had been a conflict for me, because in some particulars the world the Bundys want to make is hardly different from the one I want to live in. I respect their bravery and their antiauthoritarian instincts. I think, just like them, that our whole society has grown so regulated and policed and complicated and so inattentive to the natural human desire to live a life with some meaning and a sense of community and connection to land that it fills me with insurgent rage too. I believe, like them, that on some level America really is a special place, and I believe that much of what makes it special is an obstinate love of freedom for freedom's sake and an instinctive sense of defiance and a disdain for those who would try to control us, whether they be billionaires or a too zealous range cop or hateful little fools obsessing over who can and can't use what bathroom.

But something about this trip to New Mexico helped give me a language about why so many of these range warriors are so misguided. Because the public lands fight has never really been about land management at all. This is why most of the militiamen showing up to "make a hard stand" couldn't tell you the difference between a sage hen and a cockatoo. When they say that the federal government doesn't have a right to own land, or that BLM restrictions on grazing are tyrannical overreach, what they are in fact saying is that we as one American people don't have a right to share this land and make decisions in the name of the girl arriving from Bangladesh about how that land should be used. They're saying that her right to pass these lands intact on to her grandchildren isn't as valid as the economic rights of the mostly white men who use the lands now, because they got there and claimed them first. They are saying that we, the many owners of the land who might one day want to partake in their bounty, don't have a right to regulate the actions of the few who already have purchase on them. They are challenging our right to make collective decisions at all, to share in a national project, to hold a baseline expectation that all Americans, regardless of their situation of birth or the vagaries of life, have a basic right to even a tiny portion of all that is good and bountiful and wonderful in this country. They have a teenage boy's conception of freedom, an idea that responsibility to the future and to the needs of the broad community is a mean infringement on their rights, not a way to ensure that all of us have the freedom to make a life as best we can.

And so they use ranchers to advance the ideology of bankers, and the insanity of it all is that they've succeeded in turning this ideology into an object of almost religious obsession to untold numbers of basically decent people—the most persuadable of whom have now become the foot soldiers for the same juvenile vision of freedom that brought us the dystopia of inequality we live in today. Now their chaos fringe has marched into power, and you can bet that if they try to sell these lands I'll make my own Bundy standoff on the first parcel they sell to whatever millionaire for his gas well or private hunting preserve.

CHAPTER 31

At the Foot of
the Temple II

I spent the next three months on the road. We left New Mexico
and drove on to Los Angeles, where Dan and I both more or
less immediately cracked up again. I had saved up what seemed
to me like an insane amount of money working my job as an
investigator, and so I spent three surreal weeks there on a
binge of hotels and drugs and affairs and combinations of all
three. I was still waiting for clearance to see Ammon and texting constantly with Wes, who had just been released to house
arrest. I was trying to set up contacts with insurgent types in the
deepest corners of the Great Basin and was convinced I was
being monitored by the feds—with some reason, it turns out,
because when I later requested my FBI file, my request was
denied on the grounds that it was part of an "ongoing investigation." It felt pointless to try to reconcile the reality inside my
head with the one outside it when we went to house parties or
to meet movie people by the pool at a nice hotel.

A series of indictments covering the Bundy ranch standoff
had come down, and all over the West people I knew were
scattering or being arrested or talking about going to war to

avenge LaVoy. I tried to set up a meeting with a man named Bill Keebler, up in northern Utah, but before I could he was arrested by the FBI as he tried to detonate a bomb outside a BLM building, just south of the Finicum home in the Arizona strip. This didn't particularly surprise me, because it was beginning to seem as if the seething, paranoid vision of a country on the brink of meltdown was much closer to the reality of life than the one we were living over brunch in Eagle Rock, California. But this is what makes people crazy—assuming your internal reality is more real than the one everybody around you agrees on, and I didn't feel like I had the language to persuade friends of my version. I didn't want to seem like an insane paranoiac, and so for an outlet I chatted with Wes all day.

We were both entirely convinced that if Hillary Clinton got elected, we would see an open insurgency break out, and we were stuck between trying to brainstorm ways to prevent that insurgency and thinking that things were so far gone that we might as well just sit back and steel ourselves for what was going to come. He was also facing the possibility of spending the next decade or so in prison, which couldn't have been easy, though he seemed too proud to talk much about it or about his time in jail. The Aryan nationalist gangs had treated the Bundys and their supporters like heroes, but he stayed away from them. He seemed sad that he hadn't been able to talk to Ammon in jail, and of course hadn't seen him at all since he left the refuge, but I got the idea that he almost enjoyed meeting Mexican gangsters and Russian cybercriminals and learning about life in federal lockup. He'd been through other tests of his fortitude and mostly took this one like just another challenge. I was livid that he had been hit with the same conspiracy and gun charges as Ammon, after he'd spent only five days on the refuge and then actively tried to end the standoff, but he didn't seem worked up by the injustice of it. He'd been given a court-appointed lawyer, whom I talked with for a long time on the phone and who was just baffled by the whole thing.

"You have to understand," the lawyer told me, "that I don't usually do cases where there is a media and political crisis that's playing out. I'm trying to do as best I can for Wes, and only Wes, and turn all the rest of that stuff off. But he has to help me with that." He asked me if I'd testify at the trial. I said I had no idea if I could do that or not. Wes and I both understood the bigger problem there, which wasn't journalistic ethics so much as the reality that in the media world we had entered, even just testifying that I'd seen him try to end the thing peacefully would have looked like I'd taken the side of the occupiers, and that appearance might well ruin my career. We had learned, only slightly before the rest of the country, that from now on it was going to be nearly impossible not to be on a side. He never asked me himself, and when I mentioned it to him he quickly brushed it off. "I appreciate it, but you don't have to do that, bud," he said. "I'll be all right either way."

I spent those weeks in LA because I was deliberately delaying going to Utah. I think Wes sensed this, and I think he sensed that events and the sweep of history might be about to put a time limit on our friendship. I remember getting a text from him, lying in bed at the Standard Downtown LA, stoned and drunk with a girl I'd met at the archery range along the Arroyo Seco and with whom I was acting out an unsubtle *Pretty Woman* role-play sort of thing. "So bud, are you coming or not?" he said. "There's a lot of crazy shit that's happening we need to talk about. Not on the phone." Drake was playing on the stereo, and I had money in the bank and a full bottle of Patrón on the nightstand and I remember wanting very badly to just crash at my new companion's apartment for a while until I could get my own place in LA and find a job on a TV show and just ride out whatever chaos we'd convinced each other was about to descend on the country. "I think we have a role to play," he texted. "Like this is stuff that could end up in a civil war."

This will sound odd to some people. During the standoff, liberals, especially, were very quick to argue that everything the Bundys did was just silly theater, mostly on the theory that the government has things like drones and retina scanners now and that any kind of real shooting war with the feds would be crushed the minute it started.

But this is a misunderstanding of how insurgencies work. Armed politics functions as a demonstration of conviction, a statement that some group believes so strongly in a cause that they're willing to go to prison, kill, or die for it. I spent a lot of my twenties very close to armed politics in Northern Ireland, which was halfway an exploration into the Pogue family roots and halfway a dark and digressive continuation of my white-male search for a sense of cultural belonging that didn't involve right-wing American tribalism. And one thing you learn in the social clubs and safe houses of West Belfast and South Armagh is that the currency of insurgencies isn't political power or popular support, in the traditional sense of building a broad constituency for a set of policies. Their currency is death. Killing an enemy proves the reality of your cause, and when a believer dies at the hands of the state, it's the highest proof possible of the conviction that drove him to be willing to die in the first place. This is what wins concessions. And this is why all insurgent groups—from the Irish Republican Army to ISIS to the Bundys—develop a cult of martyrdom, which is exactly what grew up around LaVoy after the shooting. His death sealed the cause in blood. New believers angry over LaVoy's death held scores of rallies in those months, from rural Washington, to Columbus, Ohio, and all the way east to Key West—and it's worth remembering that there's a history of right-wing extremists in this country letting their anger incubate slowly. The Oklahoma City bombing came two years to the day after the end of the siege of the Branch Davidian compound at Waco.

It took three decades for the British to defeat the IRA, in a highly urbanized province half the size of Massachusetts, where a few hundred fighters using AR-pattern rifles were able to hold off the second most powerful military in the Western world. For most of this time the IRA never really bothered to hold territory or directly confront the state, because its members realized it didn't matter. A real guerrilla war in the American West wouldn't involve hundreds of militiamen trying to storm federal buildings. It would be a few snipers, men and women who are already capable of dropping an elk from half a mile away, sowing mayhem, slipping into the wilds, and furthering their cult of martyrdom every time they lost one of their own. Law enforcement today has biometrics and electronic surveillance, but many rural westerners have access to digital range finders and rifles capable of firing at an effective distance that no counterinsurgency force has ever had to face. Thousands upon thousands of the angriest among them are veterans, trained by the US military with an efficiency and expertise that the IRA and the Taliban could never match. And many of their groups, such as the Oath Keepers, have been embraced and tacitly supported by people with access to the highest levels of our government. It's nothing but a happy myth to think it couldn't happen here.

It was maybe a bit grandiose to think that we could do anything to stop this, if it was going to come, but it seemed like a stranger thing to resist trying. And since I had nothing really better to do, the next day I drove to Utah.

We had a somber reunion. It had been an unusually rainy spring in southern Utah. The planted valleys were bright green with new alfalfa, and the creeks coming down out of the mountains were swollen and angry long before the usual rush of runoff from mountain snowmelt. It was gray and drizzling when I got to his parents' house in Manti. He'd grown a dark Viking beard and looked very fit. We hugged and he said some nice things about the 4Runner. "I'm normally a Toyota guy anyway," he said. "We used to call them Jeep recovery vehicles. I'll get another one someday after all this is cleared up."

I went in and met his parents, who seemed skeptical of me. "Is this the reporter?" his mother asked. "Well, he's my friend," Wes said. We all shook hands. His father said little, though it seemed like that might be his usual way. We hopped in his Jeep and went off-roading for a bit on the hills that rose right beside the temple where he hadn't been allowed to marry. "I bet my PO is looking at the coordinates from my ankle monitor," he said, "like what the hell is he even doing?"

We went to the temple. He seemed incredibly melancholy and incredibly moved, talking about the Danes who'd built it. Then we went over to his family's farm. We stepped into a garage to see a couple of rigs he was building out for off-roading. He pulled out a mostly empty bottle of Smirnoff from a hiding place in a toolbox. He grinned and handed it to me. "This is Utah, bud." We traded swigs until it was finished.

We went outside to the family fields. "We used to be ranchers, dude," he said. "And then they reduced the grazing in the mountains and we couldn't do that. And we had fields planted, but you can't even barely do that anymore because corporate agriculture—I mean, I see up in North Dakota the huge farms, five-thousand-acre farms with three-hundred-thousand-dollar combines and shit. That's how you fricking have to do it now, and my family can't even afford one piece of equipment like that. It's like for regular people the rural way of life is going away, dude. I mean that. And people in the East don't fricking give a shit." He had an ingrained habit of softening his curses until he really needed to express something.

"And the fucking BLM is all hounding you, like you can't do this, can't do this, can't do this. You can't pick up a piece of pottery walking around in a canyon without them saying you're stealing artifacts and stuff, man. Dude, watch—I bet if we go out on that field right now we'll find tons of Indian pottery and arrowheads and everything else. They get so insane about every arrowhead, but it's all just lying there on the fricking ground."

We went and he was entirely right. "See, look," he said, and picked up a piece of worked obsidian. "Here's a hide scraper or something, I don't know. But don't let the BLM see you with it! They'll think you got it up in the hills and they'll send in the fucking SWAT team on you, dude. That's how it is here."

This made me immeasurably sad. Being at his farm finally made me understand why he'd shown up at the refuge—he'd replaced his lost Mormon faith with an obsession with preserving a way of life, which under all the craziness is plainly what drives most of the ranchers caught up in the Bundy ferment. But how, in a country that can no longer talk to itself, do you convey that it wasn't the BLM who destroyed our middle class, who left us beholden to lenders, who left 50 percent of us poorer today than we were in 1980—while the financiers and rich farmers on the plains of North Dakota and the rest of the few of us with access to capital collect the spoils of growth? How do you convey that my black friends and neighbors from a Cincinnati that's now rapidly gentrifying and who lived below my first adult apartment in Bed-Stuy are also fighting desperately to preserve their way of life—as they get priced out of a brownstone where three generations of the family grew up and the neighborhood turns into a playground for developers and rich Ivy League grads? How do you say that this cause can be for all of us? It's a nice sentiment, but then every night he, and his parents, and his parents' friends, and everyone in Manti and half the country too are flooded with the words of media manipulators telling them that I myself, my family, and the other half of the country are all part of a plot to rip their way of life out by the roots. Everything I'd ever done in my life had been with an eye on buying a place, buying a horse, settling down, and growing my plants and raising kids and living somewhere where I knew my neighbors and felt connected to the land and built a life barely any different from the one that Wes wanted for his family. But by now we had been asked to choose sides. Months later I texted him an idle comment about how more and more of my friends were beginning to give up on electoral politics and hope for a revolution. His response was more chilling than I think he meant it to sound, but to me it seemed like a perfect articulation of where we've ended up as a nation. "Really what kind of revolution are they talking about?" he asked. "A vocalized one, or a fight against 100 million people with half a billion guns, willing to defend their culture?"

It was getting toward evening, and he needed to be back in Salt Lake City by night to meet the terms of his house arrest. We caravanned together through back roads, and then up I-15, the same route we'd driven with Jon back to the refuge.

CHAPTER 32

Mr. Lucas Is My Boss

I've lost sense of some of what happened the next month or so. I know what I did and where I went, but I barely bothered keeping notes, and I have some trouble reconstructing the order of events or remembering why I was doing what I was doing. I think in retrospect that I was using a sort of manic obsession with the state of the country to avoid dealing with certain things in my own life, but this didn't occur to me at the time. I know from the booking app on my phone that I spent three days at a boutique hotel in Salt Lake, drinking cocktails of NyQuil and rum and beginning to do fully cracked-out things like burning my legs with lighters until I had huge blisters on the backs of my calves, which was fine because it was still too chilly for shorts. The girl from LA bought a ticket to Utah, but I felt too stuck in my head and uncomfortable to see her, and I panicked and disappeared from my phone and she never got on the flight and that was the end of that.

I went back to Kanosh to visit Todd and Jon. I gave Todd a big hug when I pulled up, and he laughed awkwardly. "There are some men who aren't, um, comfortable enough with themselves to greet that way," he said, but he gave the hug back and said some gratifyingly nice things about the 4Runner, and we went inside to visit. He'd just finished his farm chores, and Heidi made us a wonderful lunch with fresh goat milk and cookies straight out of the oven for dessert. We went down to the Pratt place, and Jon gave me a copy of LaVoy's novel, which after the shooting had been sold out on Amazon.

I drove on to Kanab, at the far southern end of the state, to visit with Shawna Cox. There they were selling LaVoy's novel at the counter in the local gas stations. I told her I'd quit smoking, and she asked if I was planning on becoming Mormon. I said I wasn't but that I'd been going to Catholic services occasionally and praying a lot. "Good," she said. "That's a start."

I went to Piute County and visited with Stanton Gleave, the tough old patriarch of a Mormon family that seemed to be in charge of everything in the vast county that had only fifteen hundred inhabitants. He was a friend of Cliven Bundy, and I'd first encountered him in news coverage of the standoff at the Bundy ranch. During the Malheur occupation he had signed on, at Todd's instigation, to the revolutionary scheme of refusing his contracts with the BLM. He didn't hold any political office, but he was an object of veneration in the insular world of southern Utah, and as we set up the meeting it felt very much like setting a meeting with a gangster. Wes implored me not to offend him. He was getting ready to go hunt coyotes when I got there, but we sat at the kitchen table with a box of Krispy Kremes in front of us and talked for three hours. "I don't know if it's time to fight" is the one quote from him I thought to write down. "But I guess if it is, then I'm going to do what I have to." He wanted to make a point about how strongly people in the family and the county felt about the whole public lands thing, and so he got up and looked around for a while and came back with a stack of lined notebook paper. It was a poem, written two decades before, commemorating the death of an Earth First! activist, killed by a bulldozer while protesting old-growth logging. "They are now sad," went one line I recalled, "But we are glad." I chose not to mention to him that I had an Earth First! T-shirt lying on the backseat of the truck.

I went down to Arizona and visited with Jeanette Finicum, LaVoy's widow. I told her, truthfully, that I'd been glad to know LaVoy, and that he'd been kind to me, and that I'd been very affected by his death. We talked in the living room of their house for a long time. She cried, and I teared up in a sort of closed-off and unnoticeable male way. She showed me their bedroom, his gun belt still hanging on the mirror of his dressing table, and pictures of all their kids and grandchildren. It was a touching encounter, and even after some of my reporting infuriated her she said she still thought I was "a good kid."

Wes got his ankle monitor off, and we went out for dinner to an all-you-can-eat Brazilian steak house in a mall to mark the occasion. The federal prosecutors had hit him with another charge, of using a firearm in a crime of violence, which carried a possible five-year sentence. He said his lawyer was working on a plea deal. I asked if he felt like he'd be betraying Ammon by taking a deal, and he said he'd never turn informant, but that the people fighting at trial weren't going to be arguing their innocence so much as they were going to be arguing that the federal government didn't have a right to even enforce laws on federal land, and he wasn't sure that was his fight. We talked about the refuge, and I mentioned hearing from Jonathan Allen, the English reporter Ammon had taken a liking to, about how someone had pointed a gun at the door that first crazy night, when Jason and I had gone to the office to see Ammon, ready to shoot if we tried to come through. "Hah, yeah man," he said. "I figured we'd get around to talking about that at some point. So you figured out who that was?" I said I didn't take it personally. He dropped me back at the hotel, and for a long time that was the last we saw of each other.

Todd and Jon invited me to a meeting they were helping to host, at a shiny new conference center just north of Salt Lake City. Forrest Lucas, the wildly rich founder of Lucas Oil, was there. He'd founded a supposedly grassroots rural-rights organization called Protect the Harvest, which was paying for the event and until then had mainly focused on attacking animal rights groups like the Humane Society, and trying to undo environmental regulations and humane protections for farm animals. A farmer and radio host from Nebraska named Trent Loos, with a big dark mustache and a trademark black hat, had been at the refuge as a Protect the Harvest representative, and he was there at the conference with his attaché, a gigantic dark-bearded former marine named Dave Duquette, who had also been at the refuge, driving a big trailer with the Protect the Harvest logo painted all around it. Stanton Gleave and his wife were there. We all said hello.

The scene left me almost too stunned to process. Trent Loos is friends with Ammon. He's a guy I rather enjoyed spending time with, and he ended up doing me some big favors in the investigative sideline I use to make money. Ammon, sitting in jail while reporters kept blithely repeating the official line that he had no constituency or community support, had made himself one of the most famous and divisive political figures in America. At this point, in the heat of a presidential race, the Bundy ranch Facebook page maintained by the family had more followers than that of John Kasich, one of the last Republicans left standing. Trent came to the refuge and understood the attention he drew and the fervor of his followers. He understood better than any of the national reporters that the support for Ammon's cause had been totally misjudged, and he understood that to uncountable millions of people LaVoy Finicum had become a martyr who'd sealed the cause in blood. I'd seen him in Ammon's office and I'd seen him give a speech, alongside Joseph Rice and Brandon Rapolla, at the meeting of the Harney County Committee of Safety. Trent works closely with Protect the Harvest, and Protect the Harvest sponsors NASCAR drivers and has national TV access and the backing of a man of incalculable wealth. Forrest Lucas's wife, Charlotte, had only recently made a Facebook post where she said: "I'm sick and tired of minorities running our country! As far as I'm concerned, I don't think that atheists (minority), muslims (minority) or any other minority group has the right to tell the majority of the people in the United States what they can and cannot do here. Is everyone so scared that they can't fight back for what is right or wrong with this country?" It's hardly a leap to think that in Ammon and LaVoy they found the people who would do this fighting back.

Some journalists have worked hard to understand whether or not Protect the Harvest actively aided the refuge takeover, but to me this seems beside the point. I don't have any hard evidence that Protect the Harvest directly helped Ammon. But the bigger issue is that Ammon helped Protect the Harvest. It wouldn't be long before Trent was named to Donald Trump's agricultural advisory committee. Forrest Lucas was floated as a possible pick for secretary of the interior and seemed for a while to be the most likely candidate. It's possible that he wasn't chosen simply because the transition team wanted to avoid a scandal over his wife's minority-rule Facebook post. When Trump ended up choosing Montana congressman Ryan Zinke, people like me were so relieved that he wasn't in favor of immediately selling off public lands that we barely bothered to raise a voice against him, despite the fact that even so recently as under the Bush administration the idea of an interior secretary who wanted to sell off public lands wholesale would have been almost too crazy to worry about. Selling off public lands had become the baseline expectation for what the administration would do. But this was misleading: coal production in the West—which involves much more money, much more destruction of landscapes, and much more danger to the climate of the planet than ranching ever could—spiked dramatically in the months after Zinke took over the Interior Department. He quickly began expediting oil and mineral leases on public lands, and he set off on a "listening tour," to hear comments on national monuments around the West—a first step toward issuing recommendations that some monuments be shrunk and their protections weakened. One of the local luminaries he consulted with on the tour was Joseph Rice, and there are Facebook photos of the secretary and the burly militia leader, grinning and shaking hands in the company of a congressman, under a hot eastern Oregon sun.

On January 22, 2016, the state representative for Shawna Cox's district, Mike Noel—a man who had been very critical of the Bundys but was under political pressures he could no longer control—went to a meeting and told Congressmen Chris Stewart and Jason Chaffetz, then chairman of the House Committee on Oversight and Government Reform, "What is going on in Utah has to be stopped. You are the men we have elected to stop that. Without your help, without your support, without your recognition of what's happening, there will be bloodshed." Five days later LaVoy was dead. A week into the Trump administration, Chaffetz introduced a bill that would sell off, to private bidders, a collection of public lands covering more area than the state of Connecticut. This is how you go from a snowy standoff a thousand miles from nowhere to power and influence, in one very long year.

We all went out to dinner at a steak house down the road. I sat next to Trent and ordered a rib eye. He asked if the lamb on the menu had been raised in the West, and when it turned out it was from New Zealand he opted for a steak of his own. We talked all through dinner, mostly avoiding politics, and we both enjoyed it very much.

We repaired to the bar at the conference center. I ordered a Jameson on the rocks. Dave Duquette, the tall dark guy who'd driven the Protect the Harvest trailer to the refuge, appeared suddenly on my left. He'd decided we had a problem. He'd asked

Todd who I was, and Todd had told him I was a reporter. He'd said some words about what he thought my sexual orientation might be, words that Todd was later too polite to want to repeat. Whatever he said, he didn't say it to my face. He came and loomed over me as I sat on the stool. I remembered to make notes on this conversation. "So you're the guy who made problems with my boss," he said. I asked who his boss was, and he said, "Mr. Lucas is my boss. Do you know who that is?" I said I did, and also that I didn't know what he was talking about, which was true. "I'm not the kind of guy who uses words to settle things," he said. The bartender began to look alarmed. The guy to my right, a tan and dapper nut farmer from California, sat by, silent and respectful, feeling that he didn't know enough about the situation to be sure it was something he needed to stop. I wasn't quite drunk enough for this, but he pissed me off—so I sat icily, ready to pull him into a clinch if he went to hit me, and then try to snap him down to a choke from the front, because I definitely didn't want to trade punches. Or something like that. I wasn't fully sure. He was very big, and it seemed silly not to assume he had a gun.

"You aren't the one who called Mr. Lucas and asked him all these questions about why I was there at the refuge and why he was paying me and a bunch of other shit that's not your business? Because it was a brown-haired young dude who looks like you who did it." I said that it sounded very much like a reporter's business to call Forrest Lucas and ask those questions, but that it hadn't been me. Which, again, was the truth. "Huh," he said, and ordered a drink. We all looked the same to him. He didn't apologize.

I'm absolutely certain that this goon was more or less sober and fully aware of what he was doing. I'm also absolutely certain that if he'd decided that it really had been me asking his oligarch boss bothersome questions, he would have done his best to beat me up. There's a very large part of me that wishes he would have tried. This is our country now. I decided I was tired of Utah.

CHAPTER 33

Highway 395

I drove up through Nevada toward Oregon. I crossed the Bonneville Salt Flats to the lonely gambling town of Wendover, won a little money, and turned north off the interstate at Elko. It was spring now. Ammon was switching lawyers as his trial approached. He was facing the possibility of 125 years, between the trial in Oregon and the trial in Nevada, and to see him I needed approval from his lawyers, the US marshals, the Multnomah County jail, the US district attorney, and Ammon himself. I had more or less given up hope of getting all this lined up before my energy and sanity ran out, but I figured that since I'd come all this way I might as well stop in Harney County again—because it was so remote and hard to get to and what had happened there had marked me so much that it seemed like it would be a shame to miss a chance to try to settle my thoughts about the place. It sounds horribly trite to say now, but I was hoping for a kind of closure, a sense that after all of it Harney County might have gone back to normal and that maybe the country had too.

I didn't find any. The cameras were still up, cops were everywhere, and it felt very much like Northern Ireland after the supposed peace: a community going about its neighborly business under the close eye of a quasi-military police—not quite at war with itself, but still a place where the possibility of violence lies so close to the surface that suspicion and silence have become the social baseline. After the takeover at the refuge, someone had started a Facebook group called Oregon: Harney County United!, with the idea of giving locals a space to demonstrate that they stood together and could overcome political differences. This had not happened. The page quickly gained thirty-five hundred members—a number equal to about half the county's population—and had turned into an almost unspeakably brutal and personal vehicle for airing grievances between two sides hardening against each other, to the point that much of what was said would be actively libelous to quote. Bundy supporters accused BLM employees of extortion and burning cattle alive. Bundy opponents went on a campaign to expose an affair that a married militia leader was supposedly having. Every couple of days someone would post a heartfelt and typo-ridden plea for everyone to come together again. It would get a bunch of approving comments, and then within hours someone would post something about how the BLM was part of a Clintonite plot to seize land and sell it to China, and the wars would start again. I checked into the Days Inn and then went over to the Central Pastime for dinner, because the Pine Room had closed early. I ordered a drink and one of their awful burgers and took down a quote from the same angry bartender who never remembered me while I waited. "Fuck that fucking woman," it opened. "She acts so fucking superior just because she's a fucking hippie fucking environmental bitch." I asked who she was talking about. "A woman who thinks she's fucking superior to all of us and doesn't even fucking ranch or know a damn fucking thing about ranching," she said. "She shouldn't even live in this fucking county as far as I'm concerned. You don't need to know her."

"And who are you?" she said. I said, truthfully, that my plan was to stay for a week, off-road, hunt, and fish. She looked me up and down. "A city boy?" she said. "And you hunt?" I said that in all honesty, hunting for me was mostly an excuse to walk around carrying a gun and think about my life, but that I did like to do it. "What guns do you have?" I told her. "I like that," she said, bemused. "A city boy trying to hunt." She gave me a shot of whiskey.

The next night I went for dinner to the Pine Room with a man I'll call Mark. He was gray-haired and tightly built and no-bullshit in a way I fell in love with—a former army pilot and Vietnam vet who had left the military and thrown himself into the ferment of the early '70s, working to set up a left-wing guerrilla cell in Los Angeles and funding himself, so he said, by working as a bush pilot and drug smuggler down along the border. After the revolution didn't work out, he'd bounced around the West, through marriages that hadn't quite stuck, kids who were now grown, and odd construction jobs to pay the bills. Eventually an affinity for the desert had brought him to Burns, where he lived alone on the edge of town, nursing a fly-fishing habit and a sense that a reckoning was on its way. "We're still occupied," he said, as we ordered our steaks and Jamesons. "The FBI is still here, the sweet liberals still can't admit to the anger Ammon accessed, and everyone is mad at me—because

I won't take a side." He had a sort of equal-opportunity disdain for the occupiers, the corporate and political professionals who profited from them, the FBI, and the self-righteous experts on Twitter and the opinion pages—who had decided that everything the FBI and the BLM did was right and just, and that everything the occupiers or anyone who sympathized with them did was damnably evil. I thought that if the country had more people like him kicking around, then we'd probably turn out all right. We toasted and began to get riotously drunk.

We finished dinner and went across the hall from the restaurant to the bar. Bill was working, and I was excited to catch up and hear about his hunting trip. He looked at me warily, and an odd moment passed as I realized he wasn't going to approach so we could shake hands and reconnect. I asked if he remembered me. "Sure, I remember you," he said. "So you're back." He said this very flatly.

I stayed for a week. I went back to the refuge and got chased away by a young blond security guard who drove up in a red Jeep and emerged with his hand on his holster. The river running down off of Steens Mountain was blown out and too high for trout fishing, but I got to do some fun desert driving off the back roads of the Harney Basin. Bill never warmed to me, though he got used to me finishing off my nights in his bar, and we got to talking a bit about his hunting in Namibia and his future plans. He was trying to sell the place. The owners of the Days Inn were trying to sell out too. The town felt unhinged. One night I hung out with a group of kids barely old enough to drink, who were all big fans of the Bundys and bought me millions of Jägerbombs and thanked me in the deepest and most personal terms just for being a person who lived in New York, "and, like, will treat us like humans." Another night I hung out with a Basque cowboy named Pedro, who tried to goad me into a fight for exactly the same reason. "You know what I say about LaVoy?" he said. "He's a punk. I would fuck him and then shoot him myself, because he's a pussy punk." I said that it seemed misplaced to talk that way about a dead man he'd never actually met. "Then you're a pussy punk too," he said. "Me and my friends would fuck his pussy punk ass, and send him back down where he came from." He kept up in that vein until he was too drunk to continue. Bill kept looking at me, as though to say that he had enough to deal with without me coming to dig this bullshit back up.

I left and drove north on US 395 toward John Day. I climbed up the canyon into the mountains, doing ninety with the windows down so I could smell the change in elevation between the juniper canyons and the pine mountains. I was listening to a George Jones album and thinking about all the trout I was going to catch that afternoon, and I almost lost control as I came around a bend, when a dark and wrinkled little man wearing a fisherman's cap stepped out into the road, waving an American flag.

I hit the brakes in shock and made a U-turn. There were a couple dozen people standing there, as close to the middle of nowhere as you could get, all waving for me to get out. They were arranged in a semicircle around a seven-foot-high cross formed from 4x4 steel, thickly painted in stripes of red, white, and blue. It took very little thinking to realize that this was the spot where LaVoy had been shot.

"Where you from, partner?" the little man in the fisherman's cap asked as I got out. I told them I was from Brooklyn. "O-ho!" he said. "New York City! That's a long way." His name was Larry, and he was a retired mechanic who worked a gold mine up in Grant County. It felt like a Nathaniel Hawthorne story—a lonely traveler meets a group of cultists manufacturing a ceremony deep in the woods and has to decide if they're devils to run from or if they're the people who truly understand the dark heart of the country. "Come up here and join us," he said. "We're just about to pray." I climbed up from the roadside onto the rise where they were all standing. I was already in a place where I was believing in things like wood spirits, but this was a bit rich even for me. A middle-aged blond woman with crazy eyes and crooked teeth approached me. "Do you know who we're honoring here today?" she asked. I said that I knew very well what this was about, and that I'd known LaVoy personally. She looked surprised, and a murmur went through the group. None of them, so far as I could tell, had actually met LaVoy. It was only a few months in, and he had already become a martyr. I took off my orange hunting cap.

"We bow our heads in prayer," Larry led off, "to honor a great hero." We prayed unto the Lord, amen. I found it uncomfortable to pray just for LaVoy, so I gave a piece of it to him and a piece to my uncle and to my grandmother, and a piece to anyone who would risk a part of themselves for the good of the country—which seemed like a fair way to honor LaVoy without exactly endorsing what he died for. I asked what they were doing there that afternoon. The story was that after the arrests and shooting, someone had come up and placed a cross at the spot where he'd died. At the time you could still see his blood on the snow; Shawn took some very affecting photos of it. People came from who knows how far to place flowers and flags at the spot, but the cross itself quickly disappeared. Someone replaced it with a bigger cross. That one disappeared too.

The disappearing cross became its own cause. Some of these people had traveled hundreds of miles to make sure it stayed in place. The rumor is that a Harney County sheriff's deputy made it a personal project to tear the cross out. I don't know if this is true, but it's certainly the case that everyone there that day believed the story. This time they'd welded it out of steel and planted it three feet deep with a two-foot-wide concrete base. "Listen, you'd have to chain this up to a big ole truck to pull it out, how we have it in there now," a young guy came up to me to say. "And they're not gonna be able to do that, because we're going to be camped out here watching to make sure they don't." I thought this was just a brag, but a few weeks later I read a local news story, saying that he and a friend really did camp out there for at least a few weeks, holding constant vigil. The young guy offered me a Sharpie. He said that they'd all signed their names on the cross and asked if I wanted to put mine on too. I thought so long about whether I was willing to do this that the scene became slightly tense. I finally decided that I'd sign, in the same spirit in which I'd shared their prayer. I crossed myself and said my own prayer—that we could come to a place where no more fanatic cowboys and no more innocent black men and no more anyone else would get shot by the police, though this scene had obviously done nothing to give me hope that this was where we were headed.

"It's good you're here," Larry said. "You understand that this man we honor was murdered, and you know what we have to do, how we have to drive out the sheriff and the county leaders and then all these federal tyrants. There's a war against tyranny coming, and we will save this country." I feel embarrassed, relating this, that I just nodded along with him. "Also, before you go," he said. "You need to check the airport. You'll see that the UN is there. The French are here. They're coming for the land." A few weeks later he was cited for placing an illegal monument in a national forest, and a few weeks after that he took suddenly ill and died. It's a shame. He would have loved to have seen the paranoid conspiracy theorists running the country now. I camped in the woods, had a good three days of fishing, and then drove on to Portland.

CHAPTER 34

Let the Consequence Follow

The government offered Wes a plea deal. He called me to talk it over. The good thing was that, partly thanks to our trip to the church, they offered him two years' probation, with no additional jail time. The bad part, which in the scheme of things didn't seem so bad, was that he would have to plead to the same felony conspiracy charge that everyone was facing, which would mean he'd have to pay restitution and that he'd never again be able to own or to handle a firearm. "You don't understand, man," he said. "Here it's like—like how will I even date or get married and stuff? Every girl I know owns guns. I won't be able to ride in my buddies' trucks and stuff. Like my whole life . . ." He sort of trailed off. "Guns and hunting are our way of life." The kicker was that he was going to be barred from federal lands for five years too. "Which I get," he said, with humor. "But even that I don't think they understand. *All* the land here is federal land. I won't be able to stop the car and take a leak without violating my probation." Ryan Payne had just been offered a twelve-year sentence and pleaded guilty. I told him I thought it'd be crazy not to take the deal. He didn't seem to have any regrets, which I couldn't fully understand, but I think I respected it. Our conversations fell off a bit, but we've kept talking every couple of days ever since. "It's crazy to think," he said. "Like, after all this—it's really just the beginning."

The fourteen people who hadn't taken a deal were getting ready for the largest federal trial in Oregon's history. None of the five Bundy men had been offered pretrial release, and it was hard to know what any of them could have been thinking, kept separate from one another, lying in jail and facing decades away from their families. But a couple of months after he was arrested, Ryan Bundy sent an open letter from jail. I read it in a Portland coffee shop, while I spent a few days with my sister, trying to think of where I wanted to go next.

"I would like to begin with introducing myself," he wrote. "I am Ryan Bundy. I am the eldest son of Cliven Bundy. I have seven brothers & seven sisters. I have a good wife and children who I love so much. Ammon is my younger brother. We were raised on a ranch in the desert of Southern Nevada. We raise cattle that becomes savory beef for Americans to eat. We also farm and grow the sweetest melons that most people have ever tasted. We take pride in these things we produce for others to enjoy."

He went on for a moment, talking about his father, then turned to politics. "I am not ashamed of who I am," he wrote. "I am not ashamed of what we have done in Oregon and not in Nevada. We have only done those things that we have been led to do by the Holy Spirit. Things that will help people be free and act for themselves as is God's intend [*sic*] for us while on this earth. From before the foundation of this world, God gave us the ability to choose for ourselves how we will act. This ability we call 'Free Agency.' This is the most fundamental principle of Heaven."

He talked for a while about sin, and how a free society could never be built by sinful people. "God withholds his blessings because of sin," he wrote, "and the people suffer many things, including the inability to survive, or make a living, they are taken captive, made into slaves, suffer droughts and famines. Each time they chose to disobey God's direction, by their own free will and choice they became captive in some way. Our country is headed in this direction much because of the corruption in government, but more so because of our own personal choices. The murder of our unborn babies must be stopped. Our sexual sins must be stopped. Our laziness and greed must be stopped. Our hatred and bloodshed must be stopped. Our lies and many other sins must be stopped. These sins cannot be stopped by laws or force. They can only be stopped by you." Then he turned to history.

"Our founding fathers created a form of government designed to protect our rights and freedoms," he said. "It was supposed to remain small and be controlled by the people who it was meant to benefit. It was not intended to grow into a monster like the one they just had to free themselves from. Because of our wickedness, our ignorance, and our complacency, we have allowed our government to become that same monster. It will not correct itself. Only we, the people, by the help of God, will be able to rein it in. How many of you truly understand the form of government our fathers gave us? How often have you read and studied our constitution and other founding documents? How many of you can recognize when a candidate or proposed law does not measure up to the standards that our fathers created?

"Do I think our stand in Oregon was worth it?" he went on. "Well you tell me. Has it awakened a nation to the awful situation in which we are? Are heads coming out of the sand and are eyes being opened? If so, then yes, it was worth it and it will continue to be worth it." He finished with a call to courage and, in block capitals, the words to the chorus of a classic Mormon hymn:

> CHOOSE THE RIGHT LET THE CONSEQUENCE
>   FOLLOW
> BATTLE FOR FREEDOM IN SPIRIT AND MIGHT
> AND WITH A STOUT HEART LOOK YE FOR
>   TOMORROW
> GOD WILL PROTECT YOU IN DOING WHAT'S
>   RIGHT

By odd coincidence I got a call while I was reading this letter, from an unknown number. "This is Morgan Philpot," a voice said. "And this is technically the first call I'm placing as Ammon's new lawyer." He was a friendly, hyperreligious former Utah state representative, whom Ammon had just hired along with a man named Marcus Mumford to replace his beleaguered Portland-based counsel. It turned out that my request had been held up in the shuffle of switching legal teams, and that I'd been driving around the West like a crazy person for a month waiting for my visit to get approved because the lawyers I was asking for approval weren't in a position to give it and didn't want to tell me that they couldn't give it. Within minutes of Philpot signing the papers to join the case, we had the process in motion.

A day later, Shawn and I headed over to the jail. A friendly jail media handler searched us and brought us up to a compact interview room on the third floor. We passed Ammon in the hall outside, and he shook my hand almost before I realized what was happening. "How are you?" he said. "It's been too long."

I felt uncomfortable. If I'm being fully honest, I didn't really have any journalistic object to the visit. I'd ginned it up because I wanted to shake myself free of this whole thing, and I couldn't even say what I wanted to get out of it except that I had a huge amount of anger toward him about LaVoy's death and about how I felt like he'd taken an irrevocable step toward dividing this country in a way that, without statistics and polls to back me up, I couldn't really convince anyone but Wes of. And now even Wes was getting to be hoo-rah about Trump and taking back America and mostly seemed to have forgotten how angry and confused Ammon had made him feel, not so long ago. It wouldn't be long before we were having long, hard talks about whether it would be possible to stay friends.

And it didn't look like the mighty had fallen at all. We situated ourselves at an interview table. He came back and sat down, arranging a legal pad and a flexible little "jail pen," as the guard called it, in front of him. "You cut your hair," he said.

"You cut yours," I said. "Yeah," he said. "It's a little rough. It's a jail cut. I did it myself." He'd shaved off his beard and cut his hair short and wore a pink T-shirt under pale blue jail scrubs. He had lost a lot of weight but seemed relaxed, and he gave off an impression more of an accountant doing a week for DUI than a warlord facing life. The guards clearly liked him and treated him with a degree of deference that I'm not sure they even noticed and that I didn't find at all surprising. He had that effect, even in jail. A lot of people thought he was crazy for wanting to get up and testify at his trial. I thought he would have been crazy not to.

He asked what I'd been up to, and I told him the gist of it. We talked for a moment about his plan for the trial. "So in this case they're coming down into the states, they're taking the land and the resources from the people," he said. "And if they would understand and if we would enforce the jurisdiction issue, we would've never had this problem. Meaning it would've never happened in Nevada, it would've never happened in Oregon, none of this would've happened.

"Were we threatening to anybody?" he asked me. "Were we intimidating to anybody? We let you be in our meetings. Did we ever plan anything that was gonna hurt anybody or destroy anything? None of that happened. We were there as peaceful—basically—protesters, standing against what they're doing to families across this country, to the ranchers."

I asked about his family. "We're doing all right, but I haven't been able to touch them for four and a half months. But supposedly I'm innocent," he said. "I have six kids. I've got a business that is barely teetering on nothing. I've got a farm, as you know, and an orchard that has needed my care. I'm thankful for my neighbors taking that up."

I found it hard to take, this idea that all of this had been done to them, that LaVoy was dead, communities across the West were riven, and every adult male in his family—five fathers of families—was in prison not because he'd made choices but because the rest of us had forced him to this place. "Does anyone ever just take you by the shoulders and shake you?" I asked. "And say, 'Ammon, who *cares*?' Because I want to do that sometimes." I hadn't phrased this quite how I wanted to, but he took the meaning.

He dissimulated for a minute. "That's a really good point," he finally said. "I really appreciate you saying it like that, because I can get what you're saying." But this was the thing. There was no part of him that wanted to hear it. "But the point is, it will not work the way we're going."

I asked if he felt responsible for LaVoy. "Um, I mean that's, I guess, a good question. I don't know how much responsibility I should take for him. It was very simple what we were doing. I'm not the one that killed LaVoy. I'm not the one that overreacted, I'm not the one that set up an illegal roadblock. I'm not the one that tried to cover up shooting and picking up my shells and hiding all of that. I'm not the one that did all of that. LaVoy would not be dead if it wasn't for those people doing that. The reason why they did it is because they tried to stop the education."

This left me wildly angry, and still somehow unable to convey it because it was all so dispiriting and confusing. Because it was the absurd lie of all of this, the absurd lie of all the divisive hucksters who have seized control of this country—that you don't have to answer for *anything* anymore, so long as it's done in the name of patriotism and the American way of life. It felt like I was sitting across from the purest avatar of whatever dark force had made it a point of pride—for god knows what portion of the country—that they would rip this place apart before they could be persuaded to listen to anything they didn't like to hear. I had given over my whole adult life to the idea that this was all an act, that some basic American decency connected us all and would span the breach before everything went truly crazy. And I'd brought myself before him, I think, as the person who represented the clearest, hardest test of this hope. And maybe I was just so wrapped up in the mad world he'd created that I'd become out of touch and hysterical myself, but there was something in that moment, seeing his self-justification and how far his faith went, that had shaken loose my own.

A bit after this moment I stuck out my hand without really knowing what I was doing, and I went to end the interview. I said I wanted to wish him luck, in the same spirit that I'd wished him luck back when I left the refuge, because I couldn't and didn't want to summon whatever malign feeling it would take to make me want to see him spend the rest of his life in jail, to have his kids grow up without a father. The jailer looked surprised. "You still have half an hour," he said. Ammon looked confused and held back from shaking my hand. Shawn looked confused and needed to get more shots, so I lingered and let Ammon talk. But I stopped listening, let my mind wander, and I made it very obvious that I'd stopped listening. It took me maybe longer than it should have to realize this—but there's a point when trying too hard to listen to someone who has no plan on listening back stops feeling like a search for understanding, and starts to feel like surrender. We're all learning this now.

Epilogue

Wes decided not to go to trial and took a felony plea deal. This ended up being a decision he'll turn over in his mind for the rest of his life, because, in October 2016, Ammon, Ryan, Shawna, David Fry, and Neil Wampler, along with a couple others I hadn't met, were acquitted—to the shock of all but the most faithful—of a suite of gun and conspiracy charges covering what happened in Harney County that could have put them in prison for decades. Inside the courtroom, one of Ammon's lawyers, heady with triumph, shouted at the judge to release him and Ryan, who were still facing charges over the Nevada standoff, along with the rest of the acquitted defendants. The lawyer was eventually tackled, tased, and arrested. Outside, a crowd of a hundred or so supporters burst into jubilation and chanted "Praise god, praise god, praise god."

This was only the start of a slow-motion prosecutorial disaster, though it would take months before that became fully clear. After the first acquittal, Ammon and Ryan were sent to Nevada to await their second trial. All the Bundys were still being kept on pretrial detention, despite the existence of secret

FBI threat assessments that indicated the family was unlikely to actually engage in violence. In Oregon the government won convictions again Duane Ehmer and Jason Patrick, along with two other defendants, in a second trial over what happened at the refuge, but only two of those four were convicted of participating in a conspiracy, and none of them were convicted of all the charges they faced. Jason was even acquitted of possessing a firearm in a federal facility, which seems like it ought to have been an easy enough case to prove.

A theme was emerging. At least to some degree juries and judges were able to countenance the Bundy line that they had been, as Ammon had said in jail, "peaceful—basically—protestors" airing real grievances, and prosecutors in both Oregon and Nevada seemed blindsided by how both judges and juries seemed willing to at least take under advisement a picture of the federal government as an aggressor and malefactor. The prosecutors kept walking into traps of their own devising. They wildly underestimated the Bundys' tenacity, legal savvy, and personal charisma. They engaged—at least in Nevada—in naked misconduct by withholding evidence from the defense. And they pursued charges that were vague, hard to prove, and in some cases seemed to have been a show of government force. The nineteen people listed in the Nevada indictment—even the relatively pacific Mel and Dave Bundy—were all charged with "Assault on a Federal Officer" and of using a gun in the commission of a "Crime of Violence." The charges may have fallen under the statutes, but they still required a layman to do some mental gymnastics. What exactly constituted the "assault" and the "violence," when it looked very much like the government was also claiming that its restraint and forbearance was what prevented a violent assault from taking place? What about the people who hadn't been carrying guns?

The prosecutors also seemed to suffer from an idea—an idea that had by then become very antiquated—that Americans could be expected to give their government the benefit of the doubt. The first Oregon verdict set off a minor national media storm about how unlikely it would have been for defendants who were not white to have been acquitted in anything like similar circumstances. This was a fair point, but it obscured somewhat how the prosecution seemed to think it could win simply by showing up. "Do these folks even know what it took to arrive at a verdict on any one of these counts?" one juror later asked the *Oregonian*. "How could twelve diverse people find such agreement unless there was a colossal failure on the part of the prosecution?"

I went with a photographer friend back to Utah before the start of the Bunkerville trials. We met up in Moab with Steve, the builder of the limousine truck we'd driven down to Utah in, who was there with a fleet of his massive rigs. He'd had a severe falling-out with Todd and Jon, and in his anger at Ammon over the standoff he had morphed into an unlikely public lands activist. He railed against the range-warrior types and lectured my friend about the outrages of the Bundys while absentmindedly driving her in his rock crawler up and down sandstone faces that seemed too sheer for a cat, much less my Toyota, to handle. But he had me follow and I did all right.

Wes joined us, and he and Steve seemed endearingly nervous about reconnecting. They were both worried that after

Steve's big switch politics would come between them. But minutes after they'd said hello they were waving their arms and talking about trucks and life in the exhausting manic flow they both could sustain for hours. They ended up going on a trail in one of Steve's custom six-door Jeeps and staying out until the middle of the night, and by the end of the weekend Steve had hired Wes, who was living in Salt Lake, working roofing jobs and awaiting sentencing, to come work in his shop.

We went up to Kanosh and visited with Jon and Todd and their families. We stayed at Bob's motel and rode horses, spent a day soaking in the hot pots, worked on my woeful handgun shooting, and generally had a grand old time. We went up to Delta, Utah, to visit with Dave Bundy's wife, Marylynn. It was a very trying interview. She was very nice to us and very torn up, trying to get dinner on the table and deal with her kids while fielding questions and crying intermittently as she talked about what it was like to have a husband in pretrial detention. We drove down to San Juan County and passed through the new Bears Ears National Monument—which Barack Obama had just created in one of the most militant counties in the state—and then on to Vegas and out to the Bundy ranch, where Carol and Ryan's wife, Angie, received us, with some suspicion, on the lawn while a riot of children played everywhere. Cliven called and asked that we be taken around to see the place, and so we met some of the cattle and drove about looking at wildflowers and stock tanks on a beautiful, hot, spring day. "We live for our phones," Angie said. "Every moment, just terrified you'll miss a call from him."

On April 24, 2017, the verdicts in the first trial over the

Nevada standoff came down. The jury deadlocked on charges against four people, among them E. J. Parker, the I-15 sniper who'd been so friendly to us at the Sugar Pine standoff. Two others were convicted, including a sorry and shambolic minor figure named Greg Burleson. He had drunkenly incriminated himself to FBI agents who had claimed to be journalists producing a documentary and who managed to con a great number of Bundyites, including Ryan and Ammon, into talking to them. He got sixty-eight years, the first heavy sentence a prosecution had managed to win.

The government retried E. J. and the other three they'd been unable to convict, and again the jury deadlocked. E. J. soon plead to a single misdemeanor count and walked free. He went home to Idaho and made a visit to the Idaho House of Representatives. When a legislator introduced him from the floor, a portion of the chamber burst into applause, which continued long enough that the speaker had to gavel the place back to order.

This all meant that the big show, the trial of the so-called "most culpable" four figures in the Nevada case—Ammon, Ryan, Cliven, and Ryan Payne—began under something of a pall, and never really got going before it fell apart. The Bundys had been planning to argue that they'd always wanted to be nonviolent and that they'd called in the militias because they'd felt threatened by "snipers" around the house, by heavy surveillance, and by a BLM that treated the roundup like a military assault. The government said that this was all just militialand fantasy and repeatedly argued against motions requesting video surveillance feeds, FBI threat assessments that concluded the family was unlikely to use violence, and reports of snipers moving around the ranch. But all of those pieces of evidence did exist and none had been turned over to the defense before trial. Then a whistleblower report from a BLM investigator emerged, which accused the prosecution of doing everything possible to hold back exculpatory evidence and alleged what amounted to BLM vendetta against the family, accusing officers of anti-Mormon bias and saying that Dan Love had wanted to "command the most intrusive, oppressive, large scale, and militaristic trespass cattle impound possible." The whole thing was sickening. It made everything the Bundys had been saying about an out-of-control police state look pretty reasonable. "The government's conduct in this case was indeed outrageous," the judge said as she dismissed the case. "There has been flagrant misconduct, substantial prejudice, and no lesser remedy is sufficient."

The prosecution quickly appealed, but there was no mistaking the fact that the Bundys had won a clear victory, and that, even if the judge reconsidered and allowed some charges to go forward, the case would be impossible to rebuild entirely. I found this almost impossible to process. Mel and Dave were still awaiting trial. LaVoy was dead. Greg Burleson had got almost seventy years. Duane Ehmer had decided to ride Hellboy a thousand miles to California to check himself into prison, and if Facebook was any guide he was having a hard, lonely trip. But Ammon and Ryan and Cliven walked out to a heroes' welcome without getting stuck with so much as a parking ticket. By then I was living a hermit-like existence on a hill south of Santa Fe, fishing and off-roading and mostly feeling tired and done with the whole saga. When the news came down I went off to camp to think things over. But even after a hard day of fishing and hiking it still took a good deal of wine to get to sleep that night. I stayed up, as the temperature dropped to twenty-five degrees, my mind racing, looking without luck for a shooting star.

I was glad to think that someone—be it the Bundys or anyone else—had been able to win in a system designed so precisely to crush defendants into acquiescence, one where government agents could without consequence pose as journalists and could post snipers around a home without serving a warrant, where prosecutors could use the threat of cruelly extravagant minimum sentences and the physical and emotional misery of pretrial detention to bully untold numbers of less famous defendants into taking plea deals. It was enough to make you think that maybe angels really were looking out for them. "I am so angry about the abuse that is going on in these jails," Lisa Bundy said in a video after Ammon and Ryan were apparently sent to solitary for refusing to be strip-searched. "It's not just because of my husband. . . . We hear about it and in my mind I thought, 'Well, probably they deserved it.' But you know what? I have a different outlook now." It looked for a moment like they were learning that white westerners are not the biggest victims of government tyranny in this county.

To my mind, much of the anger in the West derives from the sense of shock and betrayal felt when America's police culture and unfeeling superstructure of petty but unavoidable rules and regulations suddenly descended on a group of rural people who—by working on the land in in small, close communities—had avoided the full experience of grim cops and a life governed by the fine print on credit card statements and medical bills for much longer than the rest of us. Part of me will always admire the Bundys for their sheer defiance of a world that none of us really wanted.

But the inverse of this leads to a dissillusioning thought: the Bundys and their supporters apparently did not care to notice that the same system that had almost managed to crush them also crushes many thousands of other anonymous, mostly nonwhite families every year. The tenor of the militia movement had become even more race-tinged and tribal while the Bundys had been in jail and Trump had been in office, and it seemed almost ridiculous now to hope that anyone in their movement had much desire to learn from the experience and build bridges. My Facebook feed had begun to fill up with dark warnings about Hispanic gangs and civilizational war against Islam, and it was depressing if not very surprising to see how many antigovernment warriors had suddenly reimagined themselves as vigilantes in service of the same federal government they'd so recently risen up against. Even Wes started to share the racially tinged memes and had developed a sudden and disquieitng level of pride in his Scandanavian roots. On December 4, as the trial was falling into chaos, Donald Trump went to Utah and ordered that two national monuments—Grand Staircase-Escalante and the new Bears Ears—be shrunk, by more than half in the case of the first and by 85 percent in the case of the second. It was hard to see this as a move to help out struggling ranchers, since the Bears Ears designation had permitted continued grazing but blocked new mining and

drilling. But it was a two-part signal, to both aggrieved westerners and to big resource producers, that he was listening and
on their side. In a more diffuse way it seemed designed to help
ease the hesitant into the Trump brand of politics: the Bears
Ears designation had been pushed for by a coalition of native
tribes, and seems to have been virulently opposed by most of
the county's white population. The nakedness of the racial
politics was almost unbelievable—just one more time in two
and a half centuries of America's history when pushing back
against government overreach just happened to look very much
like standing up for particularly white economic interests.

Now the most extreme fringe of the movement had been
vindicated, which is alarming to think about, given that the
basic long-term game the right has been playing since Nixon
has been to push the bounds of acceptable politics ever further
toward the edge, something that has worked because it has
been part of a coherent and consistent vision—to enlist angry
white people to vote and agitate in the interests of a business
class that will apparently stop at nothing to tear down any
kind of shared public good in this country. The tactic of armed
politics, in service of the idea that the government didn't have
the barest right to defend the collective interest on public
lands, had now been tried, and on balance it had worked
pretty satisfactorily. The Bundy cattle were still roaming merrily on federal land, twenty-five years after Cliven sent the letter canceling his contracts. Wes and I had a darkly humorous
moment imaging the scene that would develop if the BLM
came in and tried to round them up now. It would look like a
revolution.

The Trump administration made clear that it had no interest in another roundup, which meant that the federal government had effectively decided it wasn't bothered by a clear instance of the rule by gun taking hold in the West. The bounds of what was possible and acceptable, to at least some, in American politics, had shifted subtly—and the media outlets and political operators who had done so much to fan the rage of the Bundyites to the point of violence would only be helped in their cause by the way the trial had ended, with the government coming out looking almost as malign as the Bundys had been accusing it of being all along. Cliven and Ryan went off almost immediately after getting out of jail to preach the family ideology in Montana, at a meeting hosted by a friendly state senator. The movement was rolling on.

The thing I'll never get over is that most environmentalists and most angry westerners—and, hell, maybe most of the people in this country—actually share the basic sense that there's a way of being in the world that goes deeper and has more value than anything our rampant, unfeeling, techno-capitalist society offers us. You might be a rancher building Zion, you might be edging into your third decade as a plant-loving lost boy, but I think this common dissatisfaction is why I connected with Ammon and, especially, LaVoy—who could talk with such innocence about his idea of a good life. It's why I found myself so disillusioned at the end, with his blood frozen in the snow and the full scope of our national derangement then still only slowly being revealed. We had agreed on a level beyond words that something had gone horribly awry in this country, but we couldn't agree on who were the victims and who was to blame. So we were left enemies by default, edging side by side toward a calamity that he, at least, wouldn't live long enough to see. He died thinking he was helping to avert that calamity. I tend to disagree, but it may not be long before many more of us are seeing fit to make a hard stand.

Acknowledgments

This book couldn't have happened without the faith and hard work of John McElwee, Wes Enzinna, Michael Signorelli at Henry Holt, and Melissa Flashman, who's as great a friend as she is an agent. Shawn Records deserves a mention all his own. Aaron Lake Smith, Olivia Julien, Mike Benoist, Glenna Gordon, Josh Haddix, Luke Zaleski, Jesse Barron, and Brandon Harris all contributed in a variety of ways too broad to enumerate, and I'm very appreciative.

I'd also like to thank the extended Dikeman Street family, the staff and denizens of Fort Defiance, and all the other Red Hookers and honorary Red Hookers who made home life these last few years no less wild than the time I spent reporting. RIP George. And thanks in turn to all the friends I made out on the road, and to anyone who risked self-exposure—or legal or physical danger—to talk to me. The stakes for many of us over the last year have been uncommonly high, and I appreciate the trust and openness, even from the people I disagreed with most.

Finally, obviously, my family. My sisters contributed everything from emotional to logistical support, and are incredible friends and confidantes. We've all had quite a ride these past few years, through which my parents have been unfailingly supportive and good, and the whole broad Pogue/Henson clan has been a wonderful thing to be a part of. Love to you all.

About the Author

James Pogue has written for *The New Yorker*, *The New York Times Magazine*, *Granta*, *The New Republic*, and *Vice*, where he is a contributing editor. His work has been anthologized in *n+1*'s *City by City*. He lives in New Mexico. This is his first book.